KRAK TEET:

A CATALOG OF BLACK SAVANNAH'S BIOGRAPHIES

TRELANI MICHELLE

Krak Teet: A Catalog of Black Savannah's Biographies

Copyright © 2019 So Fundamental Publications

All rights reserved. No part of this book may be reproduced, distributed or transmitted in any form by any means, graphics, electronics, or mechanical, including photocopy, recording, taping, or by any information storage or retrieval system, without permission in writing from the publisher, except in the case of reprints in the context of reviews, quotes, or references.

Published by: So Fundamental Publications™

Printed in the United States of America

ISBN-10: 0-9886251-7-2

ISBN-13: 978-0-9886251-7-4

Special discounts are available on bulk quantity purchases by book stores, clubs, associations and special interest groups. For details email: Trelani@KrakTeet.com.

For more information, log onto

www.SoFundamental.com

Krak Teet (v): to speak

CONTENTS

Acknowledgments	vii
Introduction	ix
1. Slavery and Sharecropping	1
2. Off the Farm and into the City	15
3. Coming Up in Savannah	27
Summers on the Farm	39
Yarding and Gardening	43
Chores	47
Rootwork	53
Recreation	63
4. Getting Grown	73
Working as Children	75
Working as an Adult	83
Starting Families	89
5. Communities and Corridors	93
West Broad Street	99
Hermina Glass-Hill Quote	105
6. Beating the System Together	107
7. Black Savannah vs. Broughton Street	123
8. Black Savannah vs. The Board of Education	137
9. The Role of the Black Church	153
Sweet Daddy Grace's United House of Prayer	161
10. Migrations and Enlistments	167
Enlistments	177
Conclusion	187
References	193

ACKNOWLEDGMENTS

This book would not have been possible without the support and labor of so many. First on the list are the ancestors and spirits who called me to do this work, trusted me to make it happen, and provided gentle nudges and serendipitous resources to keep me going.

I would also like to extend my deepest gratitude to James Lough, Ph.D., who agreed to chair my committee even though it was due two months after I tapped his shoulder. Without him and his oral history, *This Ain't No Holiday Inn*, the struggle of writing on a subject of this magnitude would have been overwhelming. Dr. Lough spent beaucoup time and effort coaching me through the process of coding and montaging and editing all *fifty 'lem* drafts of this book.

My sincere thanks to local historian and Africana Studies professor, Amir "Jamal" Toure, J.D., whose work was one of my spiritual nudges. Savannah carried a deeper history that I could feel but could never find. It wasn't until taking his Day Clean Journeys tour that those truths were revealed. I also appreciate him for agreeing to be a part of my thesis committee and for straightening historical points that had me tangled.

Hard-cheek kisses to Darrien for introducing me to elders I would have never met and for making my first few interviews such a breeze. His support and patience as I materialized the thoughts and stories herein provided the mental and emotional space required to write and rewrite this book.

Tight hugs to Latasha Holliman, one of my best friends and favorite writers, for being an ear to my moments of argh and aha, comforting me when my confidence wavered, and constantly reminding me how phenomenal and instrumental *Krak Teet* is.

I would also like to acknowledge the elders who welcomed me into their homes without having previously met me, trusting me with their stories, and graciously okaying my follow-up calls. And I want to especially acknowledge those who have since passed:

Mr. Steven Williams
Ms. Mary Butler Smith
Ms. Madie Underwood
Ms. Sadie Green
Ms. Lula Mae Polite
Ms. Puscha-Scott

I hope I made y'all proud.

INTRODUCTION

"It's history you don't want to lose because see, you don't have too many witnesses to explain it. Most of the witnesses is gone." -Steven Williams

"I love Savannah!" is often the reply when I mention where I live. I nod because I agree, but I also know that we love the city for different reasons. Tourists love its manicured parks and squares, cobblestone roads, and giant oak trees dripping with Spanish moss. They love the Victorian architecture, the horse-drawn carriages, and the pudding sweet picture painted for them by scripted tour guides. The only things disturbing this Savannah charm are its occasional ghosts.

They take a break from walking River Street to enjoy a plate of fried chicken, red rice, collard greens, and okra and tomato. They wash it down with sweet tea and rub their tight bellies, not knowing that the kitchen is full of black folks whose mamas made those same dishes every Sunday because their mamas did it, and their great-grandmamas perfected it at the stove of one of those very same mansions the tourists had worshipped earlier.

Many of those recipes, red rice especially, came from the hands of the Gullah Geechee, descendants of enslaved West and Central Africans from countries including Ghana, Nigeria, Mali, Guinea, Cameroon, Senegal, Niger, and more. Red rice is a child of West Africa's jollof rice. Forced together on plantations in North Carolina, South Carolina, Georgia, and Florida, the enslaved created a creole language that blended their native African tongues with English.

The Gullah Geechee managed to retain more of their African heritage than any other African American group in the United States, in large part because of the geographic barriers that Marquetta Goodwine—more formally known as Queen Quet—calls being insulated versus isolated. While the two can be synonyms, there is a distinction. To be isolated means to be cut off and lonely. To be insulated, on the other hand, is to be protected from intrusion. Their distance from the mainlands of South Carolina and Georgia protected their still-so-very-African culture from being lost. The grammar of Gullah Geechee, for instance, is African, as are many other aspects of Gullah Geechee culture—religious rituals, arts and crafts, stories, songs, and proverbs. They all trace back to Mama Africa.

After the Civil War, when slaves were freed, many Gullah Geechee began conforming to southern black society. During the next century, large numbers of Gullah Geechee left rural areas for southeastern cities like Savannah and Charleston, or they became part of the great migration of blacks heading north to cities on the eastern seaboard, especially Philadelphia and New York City. The migrations continued over time. Carolyn Dowse's parents, born and raised on Sapelo Island, for instance, were among the ones who headed to Savannah in 1926 so their children could receive a higher quality education.

CAROLYN DOWSE

My mother and my father, all of them are descendants of Sapelo Island. They were Gullah. I was told that when they moved to Savannah, everybody laughed at my siblings because of the way that they spoke, so then they changed so they could speak like the other children. So I didn't get a chance to experience that.

They were shamed. When I asked Ms. Sadie Green, a native of South Carolina who's lived in Savannah for more than 50 years now, if she had some Gullah Geechee in her family, she recalled her grand-uncle:

SADIE GREEN

I would say he was a Gullah 'cause he used to live in the back woods. He cut pinewood and whatever he can and hogwood and build him a lil' shack in the back woods. Wasn't no road back there. And his hair had don' matted down. He stayed back there 'til he died. This was in South Carolina. Far as I'm concerned, he was crazy.

Being Gullah Geechee was synonymous with being crazy, country, slow, backwards, or otherwise inferior. No one wanted to be that, so they distanced themselves from the culture and replaced their African words with Standard English. They stopped passing it down to their children, and consequently their children's children knew nothing of being Gullah Geechee. Local historian and Savannah State Africana Studies professor, Dr. Jamal Touré refers to this gap in culture and history as the "80-Year Divide":

In the 1960s and '70s, if you were on 42nd street in Cuyler Brownsville, around MLK, you'd see African men and women walking to the laundromat with baskets on their heads. People who are now in their 80s say that the homes they grew up in were bilingual; they spoke English and Gullah. The disconnect occurred when folks became educated in the American system. Teachers would shame their students into speaking "good English" instead of Gullah. Prince Jackson[1] and Lt. White[2]'s generation were forced to disconnect in the '30s and '40s, as were all of their descendants up until today. We were told that being American is the way to ascend, the way for us to go, and we bought into that. Now there's a disconnect of some 80 years. This wasn't just the experience of people in Savannah but throughout coastal Georgia and South Carolina. It hit [Savannah] harder because we were said to be the most backwards. Nobody wanted to identify with that.

Listening to Ms. Carolyn Dowse recall her grandmother Katie Brown's interview in the 1940 oral history *Drums and Shadows* suggests that the divide could be even bigger than 80 years:

> I read some of the things that my grandmother said in the book and I said, "Gosh, what is she saying?" I couldn't even understand that. But it's a great history.

The divide definitely exists, however. I've worked with children in Savannah for about five years, from elementary to high school age. Saying "Gullah Geechee" and them asking what that is was devastating. I'd answer their question with a question: Where are your parents from, and where are their parents (and their parents) from? If they didn't know, I'd encourage them to go home and ask. If their heritage was rooted in the low country, I'd exclaim, "You're Gullah

Geechee!" and would point out as many cultural survivals in their speech ("ova dey"), on their plates (red rice and deviled crabs), and in their traditions (Watch Night service) as I could find.

A common misunderstanding is that the Gullah Geechee only come from the South Carolina and Georgia Sea Islands of Johns, James, Hilton Head, St. Helena, and Sapelo. While the islands were able to retain the culture more intimately, the Gullah Geechee people stretched all the way from Jacksonville, North Carolina down to Jacksonville, Florida. Their roots trace back to particular tribes of West and Central Africa for a very specific reason. These African regions were rice growers. So Africans were taken from these areas and forced to employ their native rice-cultivating skills on plantations throughout the Southeast.

Another common misunderstanding is that there is a distinction between the Gullah and the Geechee. Many believe that the Gullah derived from South Carolina and the Geechee in Georgia and Florida, but that's not the case. They are one in the same. The terms are interchangeable much like "African American" and "Black." Gullah Geechee is not a race, however, but a cultural identity; it's not something you can genetically test. You simply need to know your roots.

I often tell tourists that everything they love about Savannah culture is because of the Gullah Geechee. I don't fault them for not knowing. The Owens-Thomas house, for instance, is a residential mansion turned into a museum in 1951. Until the early 2000s, when the museum reached out to Leslie M. Harris and Daina Ramey Berry[3] to research the enslaved Geechees who had lived and worked in the home[1], the museum only shared its history of the wealthy white homeowners, the exquisite chinaware, and expensive art but hardly anything about its human property.

The Savannah Waterfront historic marker fails to mention that when "River Street was created in 1834 and cobbled with ballast stones" that enslaved Africans created it. Another River Street historic marker informs us that Sherman gifted Lincoln 25,000 bales of cotton but fails to mention that those bales had been planted and harvested by slaves. The bronze Confederate statues in those manicured parks and squares are honored, but the enslaved ancestors whose skin was bronze have only one statue and it's disgustingly deceitful. It features a well-dressed family of four huddled together with chains resting around their feet. The image was deliberately softened, "so as not to offend the delicate sensibilities of tourists..." (Monroe, 2016).

I interviewed James Kimble—a local folk artist, auto mechanic, and New Black Panther Party leader—who created a work of art to contrast the city's one statue of Africans. His Black Holocaust Memorial shows how slaves were actually brought into this country, "not like how they got on River Street." James's Anderson Street statue depicts a man stripped nearly bare, his wrists and ankles shackled.

Savannah is one of the nation's top travel destinations, yet tourists could easily spend a week strolling along the city's haunting streets and leave without a clue about the essential role Georgia's oldest African-American community has played here. But the tourists ain't the only ones mis-educated about Savannah's history. The locals are too, African Americans included. For a long time, I myself was clueless. Years of being educated in local public and private schools and colleges, all but one predominately black, did nothing to fill in these gaps. I had to figure it out on my own—buy the books, find the paper clippings, take the tours, visit the museums, and ask the witnesses. I wrote this book not only to share what I found but also to share my thoughts on Savannah's black history.

Martin Luther King, Jr. and Malcolm X are remarkably inspirational, as are Rosa Parks and Angela Davis, but we in Savannah have our own heroes to look up to, leaders who lived and still live here in Savannah. It's important to build awareness of what happened (and what still happens) around the country and the world, yes, but this education must be rooted in local history, culture, literature, and art.

I spent hundreds of hours reading, interviewing, transcribing, editing, writing, and rewriting to remind readers what was here and what is still is here before it's gone. To praise the Africans who played a role in everything we love about this city and to give a platform for their descendants to *krak teet* about their struggles of oppression due to race, sex, and class. To raise awareness of the relationships, resistance, and religion they used to survive those struggles. To reposition Savannah's black history as the basis for the whole, where it belongs, versus a historical sidebar, where it currently sits.

Note: Pronunciation of words, the omission of sounds and syllables in certain words, and the emphasis on others, play an important role in speech. Dialect in the interviews was mirrored as closely as possible. To represent the speech patterns literally, however, would have made the stories unintelligible to the average reader. Where applicable, accents and apostrophes were used to avoid misunderstanding (e.g. the *s* in *wasn't* was often silent, so it's spelled as *wa'nt*). Though *uh* was commonly used for *a* and words ending in *er*, and *da* for *the*. For simplification, standard English was used.

---

1. Dr. Prince A. Jackson was born and raised in the Old Fort section of Savannah. He served as president of Savannah State University from 1971 to 1978 and is described in *W.W. LAW and His People* as a "Genuine Gullah Geechee Prince."
2. Lt. John Alliston White, Sr. was born and raised in East Savannah. In 1947, he was sworn in as one of Georgia's first black police officers.
3. co-editors of *Slavery and Freedom in Savannah*

CHAPTER ONE

SLAVERY AND SHARECROPPING

"This is a true life story. It's not something that we read about. It's something that we lived." – Madie Underwood

One of the most jaw-dropping, heart-sinking reminders of these interviews is how recent slavery was. I'd always imagined that bloody period in black and white, as something that certainly still affected all of us but was pretty far back on the timeline. The truth is, it wasn't long ago at all. At the time of writing this, the Civil War ended only 153 years ago—four generations before my birth. My grandmother's grandmother was enslaved. For the elders interviewed here, that meant their grandparents.

Abducted from West and Central African countries, most enslaved persons entering Georgia came through the port of Savannah. These Africans and their descendants, the Gullah Geechee, were used for clearing land in order to build homes and businesses that they couldn't enjoy. They also grew cotton, rice, indigo, and tobacco that was sold for millions of dollars they'd never touch.

Slave labor and slave sales are the reason Savannah became one of the wealthiest cities in the Southeast, despite Georgia being the last of the thirteen colonies to legalize slavery in 1751. James Oglethorpe (who Oglethorpe Street is named after) and his right hand men (also known as trustees) didn't ban slavery because they thought it was morally wrong. They banned it because Georgia was in conflict with Florida, which was owned by Spain at the time, and the Spanish offered freedom to slaves who joined their military. Oglethorpe, fearing that if too many slaves escaped to Florida and joined the Spanish military, then Florida/Spain would defeat Georgia. So he decided to be safe rather than sorry and outlaw slavery—even if that meant sacrificing money.

The early white Georgia settlers were upset about that. They saw how much money South Carolina was making from slavery and they wanted a piece of the pie. The trustees promised them that they might not accrue as much money as other plantation economies like South Carolina, but they'd be comfortable and safe instead. Instead of cotton and tobacco, silk was produced, which wasn't as strenuous a process. That kept them satisfied for a little while, but not for long. They were thirsty for that free labor, so they pleaded with Britain to change their stance on the issue. Their main claim was that the South was so hot and humid that only West Africans could tolerate it. Furthermore, plantation owners from South Carolina were interested in expanding business into Georgia, so there was more economical pressure as well.

As with anything illegal, however, the ban against slavery didn't mean it didn't exist in Georgia. Prior to the ban's end, about 400 slaves lived in Georgia. Some were smuggled in and others were borrowed. Even Oglethorpe, despite his insistence on the prohibition, rented slaves from South Carolina. Ann Drayton, for instance, who owned the Magnolia Plantation in Charleston, South Carolina, loaned Oglethorpe three enslaved sawyers (someone who saws wood). To thank her, he named

Drayton Street after her. Similarly, Bull, Bryan, Abercorn, and Johnson Streets were named after men who loaned horses, money, and/or slave labor to Oglethorpe to assist in building the city up.

In 1742, after defeating the Spanish at the Battle of Bloody Marsh on St. Simon's Island, Oglethorpe went back to England. With him gone, more slaves were smuggled into the city and more pressure was put on the trustees to legalize slavery. Feeling that it was inevitable, the ban was lifted under the terms that the number of black people in the state did not exceed the number of white. Five years later, that slave code was overturned. By 1775, there were more than 18,000 slaves in Georgia.

In 1793, the cotton gin was invented on the Mulberry Grove Plantation. Mulberry was then considered part of Savannah. Today, we call that area Port Wentworth. The gin quickened cotton production by at least three times, making Savannah the third-largest cotton exporter in the South. Rice and indigo continued being economically successful exports as well. Savannah may not be as big as other port cities such as Charleston, Baltimore, or New Orleans, but it acquired just as much money from importing slaves and cultivating and exporting crops, including lumber.

President Lincoln issued the Emancipation Proclamation in September of 1862. In it, he threatened the South that it had until January to free the slaves, or else Union troops would be sent south to enforce freedom. On December 31, 1863, thousands of Gullah Geechee gathered in churches and waited for midnight to strike. This is where the traditional Watch Night and Emancipation Day church services come from. Most slave owners, however, did not honor the order to free their slaves until Union troops began raiding plantations during the Civil War.

Freedom didn't occur in one big bang but in spurts—one plantation after the other. Black folks up and down the coast celebrated emancipation, what was supposed to be the end of slavery and the beginning of a life of freedom and flourishing.

With Special Field Order No. 15 in hand, which was issued on January 16, 1865 in Savannah, black families should have each been awarded 40 acres and a mule. After the north, the Union, won the Civil War, General Sherman met with 20 black ministers at the Green-Meldrim House in Madison Square. Some were born free, a few bought their freedom prior to emancipation, and others were enslaved until freed by Union troops. The ministers came from Savannah, Bryan County, Liberty County, the Carolinas, and one from Baltimore. Garrison Frazier, a black minister from North Carolina, spoke on behalf of black folk. When Sherman asked what black people needed now that they were free, Frazier said land. Sherman agreed.

He didn't agree because he necessarily wanted what was best for black people. He and Lincoln redistributed the land for two reasons: to punish Confederate plantation owners for their role in starting the Civil War and to resolve the issue of what to do with black folk now that they were free. Problem was, Sherman gave away land that white folks owned but abandoned when Union troops came to town. After the war, many plantation owners came back to reclaim their land—the same land Sherman told black folks they could have. To seal the horrible deal, Lincoln was murdered and Andrew Johnson became president. Johnson was more interested in making amends with former slaveowners and overturned Special Field Order No. 15 (better known as "40 Acres and a Mule"). Lincoln approved it in January 1865 and Johnson overturned it that fall; it hadn't even been a year yet. That's why Vaughnette Goode-Walker, a local historian and poet, better known in the black community as Sista Vi, called Field Order No. 15 one of the biggest "gotchas" in American history.

All the efforts to help black folk get a decent footing in this world was snatched back. And instead of forty acres, black folks were forced to adopt slavery's firstborn son: sharecropping. Former slave owners and politicians slithered under the 13th Amendment and continued business as usual. Sharecroppers worked the ground and, if they were lucky, split the harvest with the landowners. Some left the plantations they had been enslaved on and found work on other plantations. Others chose to stay on the same land because the white owners were considered fair, or because they wanted to stay put in case family members who'd been previously sold away came back, or simply because they were too fearful or old to risk the unknown and preferred to stick to what they knew.

In addition to leasing the land, sharecroppers would use credit to buy farming equipment, seed, fertilizer, food, and clothing. When harvest season came around, the tenant and landowner would calculate who owed whom. Most of the time the trade wasn't fair. No matter how hard the planters worked, the books always came up short. Whether it was due to high interest rates, fields that didn't yield much, or deceitful landowners, the debt, for many, was inherited by the next generation. And if you were in debt, the law forbade you to relocate.

Sharecropping was more widespread in Georgia's rural areas like Waynesboro, Vidalia, and Statesboro. Before moving to Savannah, Madie Underwood's family had lived in Statesboro—most known today for being the home of Georgia Southern University, 55 miles west of Savannah. But ask any black native of Southeast Georgia what they know about Statesboro, and a story of racism is bound to come up, given the city's deep history of slavery and lynchings. Though nearly ten times smaller than Savannah, Statesboro boasted of producing and selling ten times more cotton than Savannah. After the boll weevils digested the cotton industry in the 1930s, the city shifted to becoming a leading seller of tobacco, which is what Madie's family harvested in exchange for a little land to farm and a tiny shack to live in.

Madie, my son's great-aunt, moved to Philadelphia more than 60 years ago, so our interview was conducted over the phone. Once the family found out what I was working on, they said that I just had to speak with Madie, because "she knows all about the family history and everything. She loves that kind of stuff and will be glad to talk to you." Interestingly, she'd just recovered from a throat surgery that had left her voiceless for more than three months. A few weeks prior to my interview with her, she'd *just* gotten her voice back, despite all odds. Needless to say, I felt incredibly fortunate to have been able to record every just-above-a-whisper word.

MADIE UNDERWOOD, 86 YEARS OLD

The way the sharecroppers were, the white people that they worked for give them a little shack to live in and quite a bit of land to farm. They give them animals, maybe horses, cows, pigs, chickens, whatever that they can raise and breed and they give 'em land to work. And the way they worked it, they worked the land, they raised the animals, then in the fall, I'd say maybe the end of September or the first part of October, it's harvest time for everything, especially what they was growing from the ground.

Everything that you need through the year, the white man always had a great big store that had almost everything in it, like a department store. They'd have furniture, food, clothes, anything like that that you might need. Whatever the sharecroppers need through the year, they go up there and get it and the white man kept a tab on whatever they needed and bought through the year. At harvest time, when the white man have sold all of his goods and everybody settled for the winter, they always came out owing the white man money. There was never a profit. You always was in debt, so that debt would ride over into the next year. And naturally it's another debt to grow on top of that debt, so little by little they owning you again like slaves.

Ms. Madie was born into a family of sharecroppers, but didn't work the land herself. Her stories are memories passed down. Sadie Green, on the other hand, recalls vividly living and working on a plantation in rural Ridgeland, South Carolina before moving to Savannah in the late '30s. While living in Ridgeland, she and her family sharecropped.

The first time—honestly, the first couple of times—I met her, I was intimidated. She's like that aunt who has zero patience for foolishness. Riding the elevator up to her apartment, I didn't know what to expect when she opened the door. The pale pink and green flower wreath hanging from her door, compared to other plain white doors, suggested that she'd welcome me in with a warm smile and maybe even a hug. As old folks would say, though, she doesn't just walk around "showing teeth." She leans to one side as she sits, her eyes are naturally small, and she's missing a finger. To this day, despite how close we've become, I still don't feel comfortable asking her how it happened.

She's intentional, I soon realize. Though her living space is small and her belongings are many, everything has a place. Her shelves of small porcelain figurines remind me of my grandmother's collection, in addition to her crystal glasses and snow globes. Rows and rows of pictures new and old of her family and closest friends line the wall. If something catches your eye, she'll ask you if you want it. As long as she hasn't promised it to someone else already, it's yours. If you can't have that one, she'll get another just like it for you. She's known around her apartment building for giving things away, whether it's a plate of turkey wings, a practically brand new table, or a twelve-pack of Pepsi. Everybody needs a Sadie Green on their team.

SADIE GREEN, 94 YEARS OLD

We was sharecroppers and lived on the plantation we worked on. Must've been bout 50 different people--yo house dey, yo house dey, yo house dey, yo house down dey. It was like rows of houses. They don't have plantations no mo. All you can see now is black trailers, catty-cornered now. So that's how the houses was. You walk out my back do' into yo front do'.

My main job was to cook for who worked in the fields and feed the hog. My great-grandma was a slave back then, and she had me being a slave right 'long with her when we sharecropped. She used to tell me, don't stay and learn one job. Learn all the jobs you can learn, if you don't be on there but a month. She don' been through that. I know how to do cotton. I know how to do tobacco. I know how to shuck corn. I know how to do the bale of cotton. I know how to tie tobacco and everything.

I tell my children that. Mama, I ain't doing that. I said 'but you need to learn.' They had a cotton patch, not a big one, down on Bay Street like a flower garden. They had it plant with cotton, and I used to take them down there and show them the cotton. That's how my kids know 'bout cotton. They ain't know nothing 'bout no cotton 'til I show them. And since some of 'em been grown, I went in the country with my aunt and brought some tobacco, the leaf back. That's how you make cigarette? Out of that? I said yeah. They know 'bout that. I kept the leaf 'til it got brittle and it just fall down.

My great-grandmama worked the fields too. Her husband, when he wasn't on the road, he would go in the field and do a lil something—pick cotton or shuck co'n, or whatever he wanted to do. String beans, pick up potatoes, or whatever. He was white. If he was short. Say for instance you didn't come to work tomorrow, he would take off cotton day and work. He was a good person. My aunt that used to work for them, they work in the field and liable to cook then.

Ms. Sadie's story is intentional and unintentional handing-down practices of sharecropping. The same jobs that her grandmother had to do as a slave were passed down to Ms. Sadie. Ms. Sadie, in turn, passed down as much of that knowledge and those skills to her children. Curt Williams's story revealed the unsavory complexities of sharecropping. It's no secret that rape was a common occurrence during slavery. It didn't stop with sharecropping. Imagine not only having a child from the man who raped you, but having to later continue working his land post-slavery, right along with the child you co-created with him. Curt Williams was one such child. He grew up working those same fields for the man who raped his grandmother.

CURT WILLIAMS, 94 YEARS OLD

> Julius Clark. That's the man we sharecropped for. Toombs County. Now, my daddy was biracial. My grandmama was mixed with Cherokee Indian, and Julius Clark used to mess with her. That's how they came up with my daddy. [Julius Clark] never turned his back on his son though. Never.

My daughter's father, Darrien, met Curt while on the job he was working at the time. In addition to repairing cars, Curt repaired wheelchairs. The day Darrien came home after meeting Curt, he was on fire. He could not believe that he had met a man who was over 90 and still owned and operated an auto repair shop, still sliding under cars, balancing the books, and everything.

When Darrien introduced us, Curt was...cordial. When he found out that I was there to interview him, he turned me away. He lumped me in the category with other "SCAD students" who come around trying to ask him about this or that, and he wasn't interested. On top of being equally in awe of how good he looked and moved for his age, I was adamant about getting his story. Perhaps I don't like being told no. I don't know who the other students were, but in my heart of hearts I knew my intentions were deeper and purer. I wasn't just trying to complete a school project. I wanted to save some of Savannah's black history for Savannah's black people.

I came back the next day to try again. Long story short, he said that he was too busy and gave me a copy of *Out of Yamacraw and Beyond*. He said whatever I was looking for would be in there, and if it wasn't to just follow up with the author, Father Charles Hoskins, directly. I finished it in a week and brought it back to Curt with follow-up questions. I don't remember what I asked first, but it spurred a four-hour long conversation with him in the hot March sun.

Meeting Johnnie Parrish was the complete opposite. His daughter, my son's stepmother, had warned me that "he can talk." That's exactly what I wanted though, and upon meeting him, he certainly went in. The fine-tuned perfection of his stories told me they were ones he had repeated at the dinner table, at family reunions, and wherever someone was willing to listen. Originally from Twin City, Georgia—"Graymont sit on the left of 80, Twin City sit on the right"—he moved to Savannah in 1956. A former Housing Authority employee for the City of Savannah, Johnnie *overstands* the importance of sharing your story with the next generation. And his sharecropping days offered yet another twist I didn't see coming.

JOHNNIE PARRISH, 84 YEARS OLD

Everybody think when black folk came up on a farm and

they did sharecropping, they did bad. We didn't fall in that category. My dad always had a almost new car, like people who had their own farm.

When they used to farm with the white man, they used to shack up with 'em. The man used to tell dad, "Coop." He always had nicknames and he called my daddy Coop. He said, Coop, how many children you got? He tell 'em, he said, "Well you can handle a three-horse farm with them children. Daddy say yeah. I probably need three horses."

That's where you hear that mule and forty acres. See, one-horse farm is a one mule and forty acres. Two-horse farms is two mules and eighty acres. Three-horse farm is what, a hundred twenty acres? So we had 120 acres to take care of. But by Daddy being a smart man, we fared well. The white man know who they can get along with. His boss man was a trucker then, and we was well taught.

We used to pick over a bale of cotton a day. To make a decent bale of cotton, it take 1400 pounds. We used to pick a bail a day. My oldest brother used to pick over 400, my next brother picked 350, my next brother he picked 250, I picked 200, mama picked 200, and daddy was the slowest picker it was, he picked 200. That wasn't none of my sisters. All them was under me and one mo brother. That wasn't including them. That's what we did when we was 'bout 14, 15 years old.

And on top of that, I didn't know white folk didn't get a chance to go to school. We lived close to a man called Martin Fairclough. I used to, when I was 'bout 15 years old, I used to pick with him, help pick cotton, 'cause he used to get hired...You know, they used to hire hands, get a truck and get a truckload of 'em and pick 'em up in town. They come out and pick ya cotton. You weigh up every evening, and you pay 'em day by day. Some of 'em come back and some of 'em you won't 'cause some of 'em slick just like people is today.

So the man had me to weigh up, this a white man, and he had me to weigh up 'cause these all black folks that's picking cotton for him. So I'd weigh up and tell him how much it is and he'll write that down. And 'long as I can remember, starting off, cotton was always $2 for a hundred [pounds]. I'm talking 'bout back in the '30s. They start off with $2 and they had what you call dew cotton. When the dew fall, you get out there early. It still got water on it, but not enough to make it rot.

We used to have over 100 pounds in one sack of cotton. But see, what we used to do to keep from going the row was so long and you always had your sheet in the middle of the field.[1] The row was so long, we didn't wanna go to the sheet that much, so what we did, we ripped the first part of the sack out and sew another half of the sack on it, so we'd have over a hundred something pounds in that dew sack. So if we picked that dew sack and had over a 100 pounds, we wasn't worried 'bout the rest 'cause the rest gon' be lighter. We used to pick two sacks that morning and two that evening. That's all the sack of cotton we picked. But we'd take our foot and pack it.

But see, we used to make money picking cotton because we was smart and everybody cotton don't come off at the same time. So daddy used to let us go pick out somebody else. And we used to ride and walk and pick out the man that got the best field of cotton and go tell him we wanna pick for him. You can easily make enough in the first two weeks where Daddy could almost pay out his share of the farm. That's why he always had all that money left.

A good boss man was based on what kind of sharecropper he had, you see, and we made all them white people rich, we did, black folks. All us was good men, you know hard-working, clean-cut guys, and we learned you don't kill, don't steal, don't put your hand on nothing don't belong to yourself, and God will supply all your needs. That he did.

Not all black families had to resort to sharecropping. Some inherited land and money from their masters. Back during slavery, others were able to earn money by doing side jobs on other plantations or by selling crops they grew on their allotted plots of land. As a result, after slavery, some of these black folks purchased their own acres and hired hands to tend to them, including white hands. In fact, one third of all sharecroppers in the south were white. While most of the white sharecroppers, also known as tenants, worked for other whites, some worked for black landlords. Roosevelt Rouse's family had a few.

Roosevelt was an excellent storyteller who took his time sharing what he remembered of his sharecropping days. A gentle spirit, he'd pause every so often to ask me for the umpteenth time if I wanted anything to eat or drink. If I said yes, he'd call for his wife, Patt to get me something. Otherwise, he remained seated in a chair in the corner of his kitchen, leaned slightly to his right, television turned low, ready to answer any question that I had.

ROOSEVELT ROUSE, 85 YEARS OLD

Both of my granddaddies lived good. They wa'nt no po niggas. One of 'em, my mother's side of the family, lived on 1300 acres of land. My father's side had 1700 acres of land. They bought them places after slavery 'cause they had them lil houses kind of all around and there was a big house. You could tell it was a plantation 'cause that was the house that the plantation people lived in. And they was farmers, the best well-to-do black people in Burke County. I heard my grandfather on my daddy side talking one time 'bout how they was raised and what they had to go through before slavery was over.

When slavery was over, I don't know what my mother's side of the family did, but my grandfather on my father's side, he had a farm, a big farm, and he had a big sto'. It didn't have no real name. They knew it was a Rouse's sto though. He was selling stuff like shoes, not no suits now, but stuff like work clothes, khakis and stuff like that. He sold that, but for some reason or another he quit and started selling like food and stuff. Them crackas[2] owed him at the end of the year and that's when they paid off the loans and stuff.

From the end of slavery on through the civil rights era, Savannah became home to thousands of African Americans from rural Georgia and South Carolina. Black Savannah owned banks, schools, churches, social clubs, grocers, theaters, and held political offices. *Come heres* (those who moved to Savannah from other cities), alongside the *been heres* (those born and raised in Savannah), found employment "as domestic servants, clothworkers, leatherworkers, draymen, laundresses, boatmen, stewards, and in industry-oriented occupations, including shipping and rice mills. Blacks in Savannah worked not only at the traditional laborer's tasks, but were also found in the professions and the business world" (Perdue, 1973). Moving off the farm and into the city provided handfuls of recreational, social, religious, and economic opportunities.

---

1. A big sheet was kept either in the middle or the edge of the field as a repository for pickers to dump their individual sacks into once full. Then, once the shared sheet was full, farmers would knot the corners together and hoist it to the scale to weigh.
2. Cracka, also cracker, is a derogatory term that usually references white people who are believed to be racists, but it is also sometimes used when referring to lower class whites or white people in general. The term originated during slavery, describing masters and overseers who "cracked" the whip.

CHAPTER TWO

OFF THE FARM AND INTO THE CITY

"Most people didn't want their children and grandchildren to know about the old days. They just wanted them to have a better life." - Madie Underwood

The Great Migration from 1916 'til 1970 brings to mind black folk moving from the South to cities in the North, Midwest, and West such as Philadelphia, New York, Chicago, Detroit, and Oakland. But not everybody went that far. Some moved from the rural, slower parts of the state to the urban, more industrial and fast-paced cities. Sadie, though she pit-stopped in New York, fled to Savannah from Ridgeland, South Carolina. Roosevelt hailed from Waynesboro and Madie's family from Statesboro. All in search of more opportunities and, as in the days of slavery, freedom too.

In addition to the form of debt peonage known as sharecropping, the prison labor system, also known as the chain gang, was another lucrative source of income for the South. Both systems constituted a form of neo-slavery. Like Madie said best, "Little by little, they was owning you again like slaves." In 1941, President Franklin D. Roosevelt signed Circular No. 3591 which made peonage systems illegal. I was personally surprised to see the year the law was enacted, because I had family in Richland Parish, Louisiana who still sharecropped in my lifetime.

Sharecropping wasn't the only struggle facing black folk at the time. Racism manifested in a number of other ways, including terrorism. Sadie spoke on some of that, too:

SADIE GREEN

We used to walk to school from the plantation. Sometimes you would see white men dressed in sheets, Klu Klux Klan. They used to burn the cross, even if it was at the church. So people used to have sticks in the yard that made a cross for flowers to run on, like a rose bush, and they would burn that.

Racism was an international problem, no doubt, but within the United States at least, it seemed like the more trees the city or county had, the bolder the racists were. The North, as discussed in Chapter 10, was no haven. It was better, but still plagued with racism. Southern cities like Savannah and Atlanta most definitely experienced racism and slavery, but if you navigated a little deeper into the countryside, you realized there that racism didn't even try to hide.

Along with the scourges of sharecropping and racism, abuse and abandonment led many of those in rural communities to migrate to cities like Savannah for refuge. This was the case the for Madie, Sadie, and Roosevelt. When talk turns to Savannah's crime rates, particularly in black neighborhoods, we didn't all of a sudden become hurt people who hurt people. We've been traumatized for a very long time and have consequently been lashing out for a long period of time.

If your ancestors were slaves and/or sharecroppers—unable to profit from their hard work, own property, or become educated—your family started off in the negatives.

Even if, like Ms. Madie's family, you managed to physically escape the plantation, the mental, emotional, and economic deficits of it followed you.

MADIE UNDERWOOD

My mom and dad, I was told, moved to Savannah when I was just nine months old from Statesboro, Bulloch County. My dad and mom were sharecroppers. My mom and dad had twelve children. I am the youngest of all. But now they only had eight because they lost four kids. My dad had to run for his life to get out of that situation. My daddy decided to sell a pig or something to give his children Christmas gifts. Well there was a white family that lived close to where we lived that really loved black people. We weren't supposed to play with white children, but they would allow us to play together. When my daddy sold the animal, the fella he worked for decided to make an example out of him. Anytime you do something against your boss, they would come at night with a group of people. They may hang you, they may beat you to death. Whatever they wanted to do to you, they just do it. But they always came in a group, they never just came single-handed. That's the way they did, but when these white folks found out that they was planning on getting my daddy, and they even had found out what date they had planned to get him, they warned my dad.

My dad had a cousin and my mom had a sister, those two got married and they lived in Savannah. Somehow my daddy got in touch with them and told them what was going on. So they made arrangements for Mom and Dad to escape and come to them so they wouldn't have to suffer the punishment. So they made the arrangement that they catch a certain train at a certain time, and they paid the railroad for the fare. And they told 'em you can't miss that train because if you miss that train--I'll call 'em Mr. Buddem because that's what we always called 'em--so Mr. Buddem would catch 'em. Anyway, all my daddy had to get to the station was horse and wagon. Well, we would say horse and buggy.

He grabbed his family together at the time, and they made the plans to make that train. They had to arrive right on time. They couldn't sit there and wait because then somebody might warn 'em and he'd lose his life. Then a severe thunderstorm came up. Now here my daddy got eight children, him and his wife, who was my mom. That's ten people in a horse and buggy. And the only thing they had was some quilts to cover the kids up because there was a thunderstorm. And during that time, they had chickens they put in a cage called a coop. They had a chicken coop in there, eight children, him and Mom, and they ran as fast as the buggy can go in a storm, and got there just in time to unload and get on the train. Well, the white man got there in time enough that Daddy was just putting the last of us on the train. They was fixing to pull off and he didn't get a chance to get his coop of chickens, so they took that back, I'm sure. But that's the way we got to Savannah.

Ms. Sadie moved for a more personal reason. Compared to Ms. Madie's moving because her family's life was threatened, Ms. Sadie moved because her own family put her life at risk.

SADIE GREEN

If they told you 'I'ma whip you, go get yo own switch 'cause it's coming', they may not do it today, but if they do it Monday, 'remember I said I'ma whip you, I'ma whip you for that day and I'ma whip you for what you do today.' And that always was it. And don't let a dirty dish be in the sink. Oh God.

KRAK TEET:

Sometimes I used to wash dishes and it wasn't my time. My aunt used to beat all. She didn't care.

My uncle used to just whip *me* though. He used to come over there, especially when he was drinking, and he would look at me. If I don't jump when he say move, he get mad. Then he started to hit me. I said you can't hit me. I said if you hit me, I'ma kill you. He said what. You know I have never lied in my whole life. She walked in the door, I said you better get yo husband because if he hit me, I'ma kill him. She said please don't. I said I will kill him. I took enough. When his chil'ren did wrong, I was the one got the whipping. Not the chil'ren. He saved his chil'ren behind and beat me. Anybody could tell him I did something and he would beat me. They couldn't tell 'em they did nothing.

One night he wait 'til I went to bed. Thought I was in the bed, but I was under the bed. Pulled the cover back. I hit him with the smooth i'on and the blood went shot this way and that way. A smooth i'on was a i'on we used to put on the stove. My word was to him, I told you I'd kill you. And my aunt called the policeman. He came and said what you don' done? I said I tried to kill him. He said why. I said because I'm tired of him beating on me so when I didn't do nothing. I said he ask a question and it's not the right answer, I get a behind cutting. I say and I'm tired of it.

My grand-uncle was in New York. I wrote him and he came. His brother, he came to his mama, and he was taking my cousin back. My cousin was older than me, and I said to him I wanted to leave too. My uncle [who I was living with] say, you can't go. I say well I'm going. I don't let people tell me what I can't do. He said I'll show you. So my aunt, his wife, got somebody to take me to the train station. I beat them to the train station and I hide behind a car. When everybody was getting on there, I got on. So I went as my grand-uncle daughter and my cousin went as his wife, so we could ride free. My uncle was so mad with me 'til he changed color.

When I went there to New York, or to Jersey rather, I was already pregnant. And I stayed. I must've been 'bout 18, 19, something like that. My son was born in '40. Before long, my grand-uncle's mama started mistreating me and my baby. I said I got to go. Me and my baby got to go. He said, Why? You don't like it here? I said yeah, but your mama mean. He said my mama mean to you? He put me on a bus, give me $300. I thought I was rich. He said, "Don't spend your money just to spend it. Find a place to live and let me know." I said, okay and that's when I moved to Savannah.

Roosevelt left when it all got to be too much. He wasn't personally abused, but he was neglected in a way that I found extremely hard to imagine. The attention that he did receive was strictly instruction: work, work, and work some more.

ROOSEVELT ROUSE

My mother died when I was four years old. She was murdered. I remember my daddy come home after out drinking shine with Uncle Johnnie 'nem. I remember one night he took his belt off and was whooping my mama. I mean he was whooping her like you'd whoop a child, only harder. She left and ran up the street to the next house where another one of my grandfather's children was living. It was his brother and she ran there.

He cut her with a switchblade knife on her thigh, right behind her leg. And she was bleeding and bleeding and bleeding. We didn't have no phones like they got now. After he cut her, he sat her down. He said, "Come on, Bam. Let's go get some water from the spring." Everybody called me Bam. My grandfather on my dad side started calling me Bam, and so that's what everybody else called me. And we had to walk a good ways, down a hill to the spring. After we got our water, we took it back and he rinsed her off. Washed all that blood off, put some cobweb[1] in the wound, and to' up a pillowcase or something and put it 'round her leg. I can't remember all of this, but I know it had to stop bleeding.

I remember my Uncle Chester coming to get her to take her to the doctor. We lived in a little house, but the steps was kind of tall. So Uncle Chester drove 'round to the back so we didn't have to step her down them steps. And they put her in the car and took her away and she died in the doctor's office. The doctor told her father, he said, "You oughta have Henry [Roosevelt's father] locked up. Henry Rouse. She got cuts all over. He need to be in jail somewhere." Said she was murdered. She died in his office, bled to death. Had to call the undertaker to his office.

I can't remember all of it 'cause I wa'nt nothing but a baby myself. I can remember, you know, the doctor told her father about it and ordered him to call the police, but he wouldn't do it. He let it go. Now I had a uncle, one of my mama's brothers, come down there with a gun. He was gon' kill him, but he wa'nt there. He was gon' shoot my daddy.

When my mama died, my daddy went to work in Augusta, but when he left, he never left nobody with us. I was four years old and she was 'bout two and half, two something. Anyway, he left us there. When he would come home, he didn't spend no time with us, and when he was I'd rather him be gone again. Me and my sister caught some hell growing up. When I was five years old, maybe six, I was already cooking for me and my sister. Eggs or whats'ever I could find. A lot of times we didn't have nothing to eat. Go out in the woods and pull up that sour grass and eat that. Crabapple trees was on the way to go to school and things, and we'd eat crabapples and stuff like that. And then we walk on home. I had to go out washing and stuff for our clothes. I caught hell coming up, baby. That's all there is to it.

When I was 8, 9 years old, I was cooking on a stove. We had a wood stove. My sister got a burn on her face right now, 'cause I went down to the little stream down there one morning and caught some fish. After I caught three or four, I come back to the house. It was on a Friday. My sister was still in the house waiting til I got back. She was sitting in there, sitting in the doorway, polishing some white shoes. She figured she'd go to town. We lived 17 miles out of town. I come in and clean the fish and start it up. Put some grease on and it was hot. She was still sitting there and the door wasn't far from the stove and I picked that damn frying pan up and I dropped it and that grease jumped in my sister face. The scar still there today.

After slavery ended, not all black folk were subjected to homelessness or sharecropping. Roosevelt's family, on his mother and father's side, owned over 1,000 acres of land. So after Roosevelt's mother passed away, determining which side of the family would get him and his sister wasn't about who had the financial means to raise them. His father's side of the family wouldn't allow them to leave, and, according to Roosevelt, it had a lot to do with the same kind of hell his enslaved ancestors were subjected to: free labor.

ROOSEVELT ROUSE

They both was pretty well to do people, and evidently my mother's side of the family tried to get us to come and live with them, but my daddy side wouldn't let us go. We used to go out there and stay with my mother's people like in the summertime when it wa'nt no work, but my daddy's daddy wouldn't let us live with them. But we was staying in the house by ourselves, as children. Not all the time, but most of the time. The house looked like a shack with one big room. Before then, we was living in a house that one of my grandfather's other sons used to live in, Uncle Chester.

Chester's the one used to do all the driving. Drove my granddaddy's truck when he went to sell the cotton and peanuts and stuff. My granddaddy could drive, now. He just wanted Uncle Chester to do his driving for him. And that's the way it went. But my mama caught some hell, man. I did too. I mean, you know, pulling that mule everyday. You see children walking to school and you out there with a mule, riding. So that tells me that my grandfather on my daddy side just wanted his farm tended to. He wanted you to work. See, all of his children were grown and gone. Instead of paying me, he figured he'd get the work out of me for free.

My daddy had a sister named Lily who come to stay with us, and that was the first time my daddy had a grown person to come stay with us and kind of take care of us. Some people say her husband put her out, some people say she left. She say she left. People say he put her out 'cause he caught her with another man. But anyway, living with her was hell 'cause all the working she tried to make you do. And a lot of men used to be 'round her. Not her husband, but just men. I could hear 'em in the bed and I was still a child. Aunt Lily was staying with us when I left home and was still there when my sister got married, and she got married young because she wanted to get out of there too.

I didn't go for it. I told my sister to tell my grandfather, on my daddy's side of the family, to lend me ten dollars. And you know, he gave it to me. When he woke up that Monday morning and I was gone, he knew how I had spent it. It didn't cost but two something to come down here on the bus. So I had seven dollars and some change left. And I didn't bring no clothes with me. I didn't bring nothing but what I had on my back.

While Madie, Sadie, and Roosevelt left for peace of mind, others like Curt and Johnnie moved for a piece of the pie, for a better opportunity. That's not to say there wasn't tension back home, but the primary reason for their leaving was to branch out, see more, do more, and acquire more in a city where everyone didn't know your name.

CURT WILLIAMS

A lot of money was made back in them days.

JOHNNIE PARRISH

I came to Savannah in 1956 after I came out the service to go to school down here.

The elders interviewed in this book were something like the millennials of their day, born into a new century that was brimming with hope for nearly everyone in America. The previous generation had re-introduced the country to the world as a highly industrialized nation that could economically compete with all the great powers of the world. There was a lot of money being made in America, and these new era babies grew up confident that the world was theirs for the taking. They just had to go out there and get it.

As the 19th century progressed, Savannah's population of both whites and blacks steadily increased. At the turn of the 20th century, the city was majority black, full of natives (*been heres*) and transplants (*come heres*).

But they came to Savannah for more than just the money. Savannah was a place where black people could be black people, embracing their culture without having to assimilate in order to survive. According to *African American Life in the*

Georgia Lowcountry, "The lowcountry was a place where the archaeology of the African diaspora took root, and our understanding of key items of black material culture—their self-made colonoware, for examples—has come to light. It was also home of the first separate black Baptist church. It was the hub from which satellite Baptist churches radiated throughout the Black Atlantic, reaching out to Nova Scotia, Sierra Leone, and Jamaica. Lowcountry Georgia, and Savannah in particular, was thus a place where blacks chose to identify themselves and their institutions as 'African.'"

A good education, a good living, and a strong sense of black community were the primary reasons so many transplants decided to join Savannah's *been heres*.

---

1. In traditional West African and European medicine, spiderwebs were believed to speed healing and reduce bleeding.

CHAPTER THREE

COMING UP IN SAVANNAH

"You had to, back then, find a way to do what you wanted to do." –
Mary Butler Smith

I f someone were to ask me about my experience growing up in Savannah, I would talk about touching down in the early '90s when the city was the murder capital of the country thanks to Ricky Jivens and his crew. I would share stories like playing the Nintendo and Sega Genesis after finishing my chores after school. Riding my bike around the neighborhood until I found the house where all the other neighborhood children's bikes were parked. Taking cod liver oil and a daily Flintstones vitamin to ward off colds. Getting my hair hot combed until the age of six when I got my first relaxer, then sitting between my mother's legs every four weeks to get a touchup. Visiting my out-of-town family during school summer breaks.

Forging my work permit papers to get my first job at the new mall at 14 years old making $5.15 an hour; going on my first real date at 15 to see *Freddy vs. Jason* after walking around the old mall for two hours; spending Wednesdays and Sundays at a church that, to this day, hasn't produced the new building that it promised its generations of investors; not being allowed to stay out too late at the city fair because my parents feared I'd catch a stray bullet; sneaking out of the house to party at Teasers, Deja Groove, and The Playground; stuffing my face with garlic crabs and low country boils at Daffin Park; seeing the rapper Camouflage for the first time in person then learning a week later that he'd been murdered. I'd talk about how I got my first car, a red Ford Focus, at 17 and having my first child a few months later.

Those are the kinds of stories in this chapter—the in-between, everyday accounts of what life was like coming up in Savannah as early as they can remember up into early adulthood. I posted on Twitter, "Great-grandma nem been minimalists, been gardening, been green, organic, zero waste, tiny housing. That ain't nothing new." This chapter, these interview excerpts, inspired that post.

One of my primary questions for this portion pertained to "what used to be where."

STEVEN WILLIAMS, 82 YEARS OLD

I think city limits came as far as 60th Street. That was a watermelon patch all through there [he said pointing out his South Street window]. It was actual farms out here, which is why they called us dirt farmers.

FLORRIE SCRIVEN, 82 YEARS OLD

That's when [white folks] took over River Street. They just took it over. River Street used to be warehouses. A lot of trucks would come in with potatoes and onions. We used to go down there on River Street to the warehouses and they would give us white potatoes and onions and they would give us something like supposed to be butter, but it wasn't butter. It was lard and they give you this coloring to put in it. You didn't have to buy it. They'd give it away.

CURT WILLIAMS

The first black girl scout headquarters was on Jefferson Street. The very first black girl scout headquarters that they said they'd never tear down. They'd remodel. It was some lil' yellow houses owned by a man called Mr. Mayes. When Mr. Mayes died, he owned 721 units. Every brown and yellow house in Savannah was owned by a man called Mr. Mayes.

LULA MAE POLITE, 84 YEARS OLD

I was born and raised here. Some places I go and I don't even know what happened because they don' changed it up so much, especially Broughton Street. We lived, lemme see, it was Bay Street and Bryan Street, about four streets from Broughton on Indian Lane. So Broughton Street was just like a place that everybody was familiar with, but like now you wouldn't believe. We used to go down there on Broughton and go up to Barnard, that's where Kress was. And then the big ole' city market. They to' that market down. It was a big city market. You could go in there and buy everything you wanted. All the fresh food, the fish. They had the butchers.

The people had stalls all over the marketplace and our mama used to work in one of 'em called Kessler's Lunchroom. Then it was another lunchroom on the other side. Where my mama worked at, you come from Broughton Street side, and theirs was right there. Right there at that opening. Then it was another from the other side like if you came from Congress Street side. It was a large marketplace.

It wasn't hardly no whites selling. Black people had the stalls where they sold fresh butter beans, peas, corn, you know, anything like that you wanted. You know, watermelon trucks and stuff like that. All the fruits you want. The meat shop, Maden Brothers, they had they wholesale stuff. You can get all your meats from. There was a lot of chickens. You could get a live chicken if you wanted to. You could pick out what you want and they would kill it for you. If you wanted to buy some chicken feet to go along with it, you could buy a bag of chicken feet.

There was another lil' sto we used to buy food from called Jack Daley. Did [Florrie] tell you about that sto? Jack Daley, that was a sto, they were Jews. You could buy a whole butt of a bologna. You could get a whole butt for a dime or a nickel. And they had the syrup in something like a keg and you could go and get one of them paper bag and you could get a nickel worth of syrup and fill that bag up. Yep, you put it in a paper bag. They had different size brown bags and you could put some syrup in that. You could get a nickel worth of rice. With a dollar, you had you a bag of groceries. Things were real cheap during those times.

The primary difference, I noticed, in the coming of age stories was how well off people were (or weren't). Ms. Smith's family, for example, were pretty financially set, as were sisters Lula Mae and Florrie.

MARY BUTLER SMITH, 94 YEARS OLD

In those days, we were considered rich, colored folks. My father made a good living, I know that. My mom didn't work a day in her life, except us, her children. And my father had his own business, Butler Tire Company. He was raised in Atlanta and learned his trade in Atlanta, and he came to Savannah before he married my mother. I probably knew at some point, but I forgot how long they knew each other before they married. Daddy dealt with most of his trade with whites. He was the best there was, and I'm sure that he didn't get as much money as he should've gotten. He was considered the best, but he made a good living.

He had a car and a truck. Daddy liked Chryslers and Buicks. At one point, he drove to Atlanta with my older brother. And he was always going to do tire work around the area. When he came back, my older brother was driving a brand new Chrysler off the lot. My daddy said, "Queen, this is for you." She was about the only black lady in Savannah at that time who had her own car. It was maroon with black trim, black fenders. It was sitting up like a buggy, high up off the ground. She was a proud black soul driving that car.

Daddy bought Mama one of the early gas stoves. It was blue and white, and on the end was a vessel on the side of the stove where you could heat water in it. Very modern. It was a big, heavy stove. You didn't move that out of the house when you moved.

We never experienced an outside toilet, not at our house. Now at my grandmother's, there was the bathroom out in the backyard at the very end of the yard, there was a lane, to the end was the toilet. You had to get out there. They would pull chains. It was just outside of the house. It wasn't a part of the house. It was a built outside with a chain to pull to flush it. They had pipes running like that. So you weren't building up any mess out there. Then finally they got the inside toilet.

You had chamber pots with a top on it. You had to cover it and you kept it under the bed at night and if you had to use the bathroom then you had to use the chamber pot. Then you take it out and empty it in the outhouse in the morning. This was before we had bathrooms in the house. Rich folks had chamber pots.

You did what you had to do with what you had.

FLORRIE SCRIVEN

Our mom was a cook. They had the farmer's market where the City Market is now. It used to be a market there with all the Afro-Americans. They had like stalls in it where they sold vegetables, and there were a couple Caucasians that was in that particular building, but they had the Kessler's restaurant in there. And that's where my mom, my mom's sister, my mom's auntie, her children, and all of my cousins worked.

LULA MAE

My dad was a longshoremen. That was the top job back then. That and maybe the mail carriers and they had the sugar refinery, which was a pretty stable job also.

Mr. Steven Williams, who worked for the International Longshoreman's Association (ILA) for more than 20 years, agreed about longshoremen, those who load and unload ships at the port, being the top job back then—nearly verbatim.

STEVEN WILLIAMS

> It was the best job a black man in this city could have then. Still is.

For context, the ILA self-proclaims to be the largest union of maritime workers on the continent of North America, currently representing more 65,000 longshoremen. If you work as a longshoreman in Savannah, you have no choice but to be in the union. Savannah's branch of that huge organization is numbered ILA 1414. The port brings billions of dollars into the city every year, and the workers are paid relatively well for it. As Mr. Williams pointed out, it's a top job for black men in Savannah, even today. On any given day, you can drive down to the port and see hundreds of TWIC[1] cards in the air, hoping for a chance to be chosen for the day. Because they know that if they get chosen, then they have a chance to prove their worth, obtain a more permanent position, and start rolling in the dough.

I remember being invited to a longshoreman's ball once and because I'd never heard of it before, I asked around about it. Someone shared that that's where the single women go who are looking for a man with money. When Ms. Lula Mae shared that some women used to stand around waiting for ships back in the day, it sounded hilariously familiar.

LULA MAE POLITE

> The ships used to come in. The longshoremen ships, but they used to call 'em something else then. When those ships come in with the sailors, white sailors too, they would dock and come up on Indian Street. There were houses down there they called the big houses where the girls would be. They'd go to have a good time. It was a bar right on the corner of Indian and Fahm. His name was Joe Simms. He had a bar where the sailors would go and drink. And up Indian Street, on Indian and Ann, his sister, Lillian Simms, she had a restaurant and the girls--white girls and black girls--and they would, the sailors would go there. There was some mo' houses with the black people, they called 'em the big houses. They would be out there, honey. When them ships came in, they was really waiting on 'em.

Mr. Williams was one of the lucky ones to have been chosen and, like most of the chosen ones, he stayed until he retired. He shared with me a plaque of the retirement letter he'd written for ILA 1414, Savannah's branch of the union:

> In the middle sixties, I came to the Longshoreman Hall from a job paying one ($1.00) per hour with no benefits and I was truly amazed that I could earn $2.96 per hour plus have benefits. I was even more amazed that I could ask a BLACK MAN for a job and if I had a problem with that job I could complain to a BLACK OFFICIAL. This of course was the greatest moment of my life.

Ms. Lula Mae also pointed to mail carrying being a good paying job *black in the day*. According to Pastor Southall Brown Sr., though, working for the post office wasn't all that hot of a job.

PASTOR SOUTHALL BROWN SR., 95 YEARS OLD

My daddy worked for the US Postal Service. We grew up thinking we were rich because nobody never told us we were poor little black children. My daddy also owned two tenement houses—519 and 521 Hartridge Street, a short street between East Broad and Price, right next to Gaston. It was a four-room house, but my daddy added a big family room that he built himself. I remember I used to sleep back there, and there was a bedroom, a kitchen, a bathroom.

Now I was born there and we lived there until my daddy hemmed to a community that was where...what's the word I want...whites used to live, which happens to be Victory Drive. White people lived from West Broad of Martin Luther King down to Florence. That's the first cross street. Black people lived from Florence down to Hopkins. That's where the light is. Nobody lived down there where Bishop Grace is, nobody. All that was a big ball field.

Ms. Lula Mae noted that the sugar refinery (Savannah Food and Industries[2]) was another stable job, and there were a couple interesting stories about the refinery.

CURT WILLIAMS

Like sugar refinery. That was a slave's camp almost. See black folk, up until many years, everybody that worked to the sugar refinery had to stay on they grounds in lil' ole' houses. You wasn't nothing but a house nigga to that white man. You always got the nigga that fix the bed and fix the food. That's the house nigga. He'll come out there to the lil shack and...one of 'em still living. He come by here sometimes. He'll say, "I was a fool. Nobody likes me." And he's a member of St. Paul. I'ma try to think of what his name is.

But you can't actually get mad with him because that's the way things were back in them days. You got to think that way too, see? They didn't know no better. Because that white man will put a badge on you, a star on you, and you better than everybody else now. See the system?

SADIE GREEN

I didn't work for the sugar refinery, but I used to go out there and mess around. The people that lived there didn't have to work there. They lived around. Like, I live here. But people would think, I would be living in that house. A restaurant used to be right there and we used to go there and get french fries and stuff. And so that's how that was. It was houses on the land, but they had that to rent out. Put it like this: If you out of town and you and yo family need some place to stay, then you could rent an apartment from them and work there. You came to Savannah to work there. Like you come to Savannah to go to school. That's how it was. Wasn't no difference.

The sugar refinery has a history of building houses and communities for its employees. In 1908 in its home state of Texas, Imperial Sugar "set up a support system for employees including building 500 new homes, providing medical care, and establishing the Imperial State Bank, the Imperial Mercantile Company, a company store, various retail stores, a cotton gin as well as feed and paper mills" (Imperial Sugar Company, 2019).

How much money refinery employees actually made, I don't know, but no one disputed that it paid well in comparison to other warehousing jobs in the city. While there was only a handful of jobs that paid living wages, hundreds more paid next to nothing. The parents of Ms. Madie and Mr. Steven Williams, for instance, struggled to make ends meet.

MADIE UNDERWOOD

And lemme tell you, this was so funny to me, I always laugh about this part. That was the first words I learned how to spell: For Rent. We was little kids out in the street, you know, and other little kids would tease us. And so what we did, we made a song out of it and a dance. And we'd say, "F-O-R-R-E-N-T." We'd be out there dancing and singing it, so poor and ignorant, not knowing we was getting put out 'til we was moving.

STEVEN WILLIAMS

My family was dirt po. I can remember the wooden containers outside that you throw trash in. I can remember people going in there and getting stuff and washing it off. I can remember my mama washing meat off and boiling it and then cooking it. And you could almost taste it while you was eating it. But if you was hungry, you ate it. You don't have to show a hungry man a menu, right?

I had three brothers. We had to wear each other's clothes. You couldn't claim no ownership. I remember one time I spent about four weeks laying away a pair of pants, and then I got the pants but I didn't have time to put 'em on yet. Then I saw my brother walking down the street and I remember wondering why he had those pants on because I had 'em on layaway. I saw my own pants walking down the street. I can laugh now, but it wasn't funny then. In other words, you put on whatever was there. You couldn't have no argument about it because mama said what's his is yours and what's yours is his. That's how we survived.

---

1. A TWIC card is a Transportation Worker Identification Credential required by the federal government for workers accessing secure areas of the port.
2. Savannah Foods & Industries opened in 1915, marketing its sugar products as Dixie Crystals. The company was purchased by the Imperial Sugar Company in 1997. Locals, however, simply referred to it as "the sugar refinery."

SUMMERS ON THE FARM

Regardless of how rich or poor they grew up, there were many similarities in how they were raised. Visiting family in the country is one of them. This might be a foreign concept to some, and as a southerner through and through I didn't even realize this until I spoke with friends in Washington D.C. who considered all of the south as the country. Within the south, there are the city/urban areas and then you have the country/rural areas. Those rural areas are where we would visit.

It was my grandmother leaving Monroe, Louisiana to visit her relatives on the farms in Rayville, Louisiana. It was Ms. Ruby leaving Savannah for Darien, Ms. Smith heading to South Carolina, Pastor Brown going to his mother's hometown of Columbia, and Lula Mae going to Montieth. Before the days of keeping in contact with family through telephone and Facebook, you had to get down there. Not just for family reunions, but throughout the year. If you had kids, you dropped 'em off in the country. I'd assume it was to probably get a break as a parent, too, but to more importantly show them where they came from and instill in them the value of hard work through the laborious task of working the land as well as preparing and preserving food in true DIY fashion.

RUBY JONES, 91 YEARS OLD

My mother would take us in the country when school closed. We was glad when summer come. We would go in the country to her people in Darien. When you come back from the country, them people give you so much because they have so much on them farms. Give us chickens, peaches, okra, tomato, pears. At the time I didn't like okra. I like okra now. We had bushels of pears, those hard green pears, and you peel all those things and my mother used to preserve 'em in jars with the red, rubber thing on top of 'em. She didn't teach us, she did it, but I know she put 'em in pots with some sugar. But we had to peel 'em. Then put 'em in the pantry or someplace where it's cool.

MARY BUTLER SMITH

My mother was a Carolinian, and I think it was six of them. Three of them had big farms over there in South Carolina. When we'd go there to visit, she'd put us to work. She would put *them* to work. I wasn't going to no field to pick no corn. But when it came to the watermelons, we'd pick 'em up and drop 'em, what we called 'bust 'em' and scoop the meat out. That was the best watermelon. And I remember that.

PASTOR SOUTHALL BROWN SR.

My daddy was from the city of Savannah and my mother was from the city of Columbia. They used to put tags on us—Matthew Brown, Columbia, South Carolina—and give it to the conductor on a train and then he would put us out in Columbia and we'd visit our grandparents.

LULA MAE

We used to go when school closed and spend the summer with them out in Montieth. We never asked about slave days though. Never talked about that. She was tall and hefty and wore the skirt and thing way down here. My grandmother used to work for a man name Mr. Waiters. He was a black man and he was over the rice farms. They used to go and work in the rice farms. That's when I found out that rice is grown in water. We used to go down there. And my great-grandmother, she used to fix the lunch and put it in this bucket and me and my cousin used to go and take my grandmother the lunch. She used to wear these boots way up here in the water. I say what she doing in the water and she work in the rice place. And they say that's where the rice grow at, in the water. I say that's strange.

I remember all of my great-grandparents, except on my Daddy side. His mama, I can just vaguely remember her. She was stout and had this lil church, but other than I don't know. But my granddaddy now. We was buddies, on my daddy side. He would come and stay with us and he like to drink too. My uncle used to make shine. He used to like to buy this meat they call it sous meat now, but they used to call it hog head cheese. And he would send me to get that and I would pick the corn on his toe. He used to sit and eat that hog head cheese and when he finished eating that, he would go to sleep in the chair. He be don' knocked out.

I remember my grandmama bed used to be so high and they used to make they own mattress out of straw and something they called ticking. It's the mattress cover. You put it in there and sew it all around, just like a mattress. That thing used to be so soft. My grandmother died right there in Indian Lane. She was sick, and my mama went and got her and brought her brought her to stay with us. My grandmama, before she died, had a po'ch on her house. And she had a big ole' peach tree out there and plum trees. It was a lot of shade 'round her house. She had a well to get the water out. My grandmama she used to cook on a stove. But my great-grandma she used to cook on a fireplace. She had this iron pot. You might seen these cowboy movies with that big ole cast iron. She used to cook what she called tun mush. I think it was oatmeal. That's all she used to cook. She'd put some butter on it and eat that. Now my grandma used to do the cooking, my mama's mama. They had a house they called a smoke house. That was some delicious bacon used to be hanging up in there with the ribs on it.

She had calf and she had a cow. One of the calf, and she had a bull. And that bull ain't paid nobody no attention but my Uncle Ben. And he told me to hold that bull for him one time, and I hold the bull and the bull stuck me right here. He tied that bull up to that tree and he put a beating on that bull. He beat that bull a while. I said I won't hold 'em no more. That was in the country. They call it Rice Hope now, out in Port Wentworth.

YARDING AND GARDENING

We didn't wait until those country visits to get fresh produce from their farms, though. Gardens were kept in Savannah too. Gardening is a long time tradition of black folk, beginning in Africa and following its people across the diaspora. My grandmother maintained gorgeous gardens at her Louisiana home. She kept flowers in the front—sunflowers, I recall most vividly, almost as tall as me—and rows of tomatoes, okra, and collards in the back. I also remember my grandmother bartering some of her crops, or just sharing with neighbors. I recall some of those neighbors putting objects other than fruit, vegetables, and flowers in the gardens, like little resin statues, bottle trees, and makeshift sitting stools.

Gardens kept the family fed at a much lower cost than the grocery story, provided healing for ailments, were a beautiful source of community building, and indirectly told stories. "How a society organizes itself spatially and utilizes space is essential to understanding how the society functions" (Westmacott, x). And nearly all of my elders had stories to tell of gardens.

MADIE UNDERWOOD

Most people had gardens where they grow the vegetables. All our food was organic food. My daddy always had at least two gardens, all the time and he never used nothing but natural fertilizer to grow his vegetables and stuff. And we had fresh vegetables all the time.

And when I got married, I was 18, and my mother-in-law and father-in-law, he had far more gardens than my dad had. But he lived out a little bit. I can't remember the neighborhood he lived in, but he lived out over across Gwinnett Street. I can go there right now if I was there. Savannah wasn't full of houses like it is today. Wasn't even full of highways like it is today. It was completely different. Anyways, he even was raising animals too. He would have turkeys, ducks, chickens. He had one horse and I can't remember whether he had a cow or not. I know he had pigs. My father-in-law had all of that.

MARY BUTLER SMITH

We lived in a big two-story house nearly on the corner and three quarters from the front of the property. All the way in the back and the front too, there were two pecan trees and on the back, one pecan tree, a peach tree, and a plum tree, and a big fence on the front of that property. All the rest of that property belonged to Grandpa—my mama's daddy, who was Cherokee Indian. My grandmother and grandfather were Cherokee Indians. Granddaddy used to come walk all the way 'cross from the west side to the east side and farm the land we lived on.

It was that big. And in the back of the property, my grandfather had a chicken yard back there where he raised chickens.

He couldn't keep a picket fence in the front of that yard. During pecan season, the kids would break down that fence and come in our yard to get the pecans. He would just repair the fence and start over. Every year, the same thing would happen. Plus, he'd had enough to where, I remember he used to bag 'em up and take 'em to the shop and sell 'em. And our tree bore fat pecans. Not them lil skinny ones, but big fat ones.

CURT WILLIAMS

You ride out there on Cornwall Street, all the way down, that big ole' 14-room house, that's where we grew up at. And it look just like brand new now. My sister still live there. I was a lil boy when we moved here [from Valdosta]. We still farmed though when we moved here. We always farmed— fruits, vegetables, animals, all dat.

Typically, we refer to gardens as places where we grow fruit and vegetables. We refer to yards as where we grow flowers and maintain livestock, but I'm using garden broadly here for all of it, as it's the same land, serving different functions. The point is to show that gardens are much more than places of leisure. As described by Richard Westmacott in *African-American Gardens and Yards in the Rural South*, "They are places where independence is asserted with extraordinary vigor and resourcefulness. They demonstrate that African Americans hold strongly the agrarian values of hard work and self-reliance" (2).

CHORES

Hard work also showed up in their chores, another similarity across class. I don't care how much money your parents made, you worked hard to upkeep the property.

RUBY JONES

Oh lord. Scrubbing floors on your knees, ironing, had to wash clothes on a rough board, make ice cream in a churn. I've cut wood, I've killed chicken, cleaned the chicken, and everything.

CAROLYN DOWSE

I said I'd never wanna see a hardwood floor. During those days, you didn't have buffers and you used Johnson paste wax and you had to take a towel and buff the whole house on your hands and knees and then you those tin blinds and you put the blinds in the tub and your hands were all cut up. And you washed the curtains and you put them all on stretches. We didn't have washing machines and dryers. We washed everything—the sheets, the pillowcases, the men shirts, everything. And we still used the line outside to dry, and sometimes the bird would come and put drippings on. Oh my gosh, or if a heavy wind came and blew things down in the sand, you wanted to cry. But we did all that. You had a day, you just got out there in that yard with that wash bowl and then you had a day when you had to starch all the collars, all the everything.

This is why I'm so structured today, because we came up so structured. We had to get up and you had to leave the house spotless, because the old people said if we have to come home, I'm not going to be embarrassed and we had to eat a full breakfast. You couldn't eat cereal. Anybody who was in my age category and you talk to them, you had grits and bacon and sausage and hot chocolate and all of that. Every morning—before the sun came up! And you had better not be late for school.

And we had a fig tree. We had to climb up that fig tree and pick the figs as part of our chores. I told somebody, my friend, I have a friend who's in my age category, we were laughing so hard. We said, you know, we were little slaves. But I mean, that's the way we were raised.

MARY BUTLER SMITH

The girls did most of the work. It was never fair. I don't remember ever seeing my brother's scrubbing or ironing or anything like that. No, that was women's work. Not back then. The house work and the cleaning. The boys might've did the yard work, something like chopping wood or whatever.

Roles were a big conversation between my husband and me when we moved in together. I was expected to clean the house and he assumed he'd do the yard work. But yard work, I quickly realized, only took place on Saturdays whereas house work was every day. We restructured that very quickly! Then again, I was grown and able to make that decision. As a child, I would have likely have had no choice.

Before I assumed that all boys did back then was the occasional yard work while the girls did the daily house work, I got a little more specific with my questions. I wanted to know if the boys weren't cleaning around the house, then what were they doing besides yard work. Where were they spending their time in such a way that it benefitted the whole household?

MARY BUTLER SMITH

> Now Daddy was a businessman and the boys grew up and they learned the business. After school, they would go to the shop and learn how to fix tires.

Learning the family trade wasn't limited to just boys. In fact, Ms. Mary Smith's family was highlighted in Father Charles Hoskin's published timeline of Savannah. In it, Hoskins mentions that Ms. Smith's father, Joseph Butler, moved to Savannah with 25 cents in his pocket. He worked at a local tire shop for a few years before opening his own in 1922. "His wife, Mrs. Queenie Butler, did the tube repair work…and his only daughter Mary was the bookkeeper" (p. 220).

MARY BUTLER SMITH

> My mama even went to the shop and learned how to repair tubes. Tires were made with rubber tubes inside of them with air in them to keep the tires firm on the wheels. And they

would run over things in the road and puncture them, and Mama learned how to fix them tubes. And she'd put on her little overalls and mechanic hat and go to the shop and work there from after breakfast until time to go home and fix dinner. I had some pictures of Mom somewhere. I hope I still have some of 'em in her overalls standing in front of the shop.

Raising boys to do a certain type of chores and girls another is an individual thing. It didn't seem to be across the board or something that most people did or didn't do. Some households did it that way and others didn't. For Carolyn Dowse, her brothers did just as much work around the house as she did.

CAROLYN DOWSE

My brother was older, but my brother could clean a house better than any woman. My brother could cook. When he got married, a lot of times, he would clean the house and cook. He could iron clothes. I mean, the parents taught the boys what to do. If your wife got sick or something, you needed to be able to do. So the mothers taught their sons. My brothers? Oh yes. They could do everything that we did.

MADIE UNDERWOOD

Anything pertaining to laundry, house cleaning, yard cleaning, taking care of babies. The whole bid. By the time I was 8 years old, I knew how to do all of it. I ironed everything, even under clothes. Everybody didn't iron everything, but I did.

We did the same thing. The boys had to learn how to keep house as well as we did, but they didn't really learn how to see about babies the way we did. But we all learned how to keep house. Whatever the house needed, that's what we were expected to do. The outside, the laundry, all of us didn't have to learn how to cook that young. Some of us didn't learn to cook until we got to be about 15. The older people usually do the cooking, but they trained us to do everything else at a very young age.

And Pastor Southall Brown Sr. worked alongside his mother.

PASTOR SOUTHALL BROWN SR.

In my house, the reason and I want you to hear this well, the reason I did not have any problems in the military was because my mother was a top sergeant and she ran a clean platoon. When I was coming up, everybody had their job in the morning before going to church, school or whatever. My brother's job was to the sweep the sidewalk, turn the broom on the edge and sweep between the lines.

That was his job. My job was to help my mama make up the beds, feed the chickens, and back the car, because my dad had that 41 Plymouth. Sometimes I'd try and skip the chickens to catch my friends walking to school. Before I knew it, my mama would be yelling, "Come on back and feed these chickens, and you better not be late to school." I'm stupid. I'm wondering how she found out I didn't feed those chickens; they can't talk. So I asked her one day after I got up, you know, in age. I said mother how you used to know. She said because when I go out there, they come to the fence and they went 'quack.' They wouldn't come to the do' had they ate.

My sister Helen's job was to cook breakfast every morning, and my oldest sister's job was to clean up the bathroom. Now when I say clean up the bathroom, I mean dip the water out the commode and they had a thing called Bon Ami. You ever heard of it? It was like Ajax. You put it in there and I've never seen a ring in our bathroom, never. That and white vinegar.

ROOTWORK

Using vinegar to clean the bathroom is considered a folk remedy, which is an herb, food product, or household item that's used for healing or cleaning purposes. Especially regarding medicine and healing properties, folk remedies are usually recommended by someone who did not study the subject formally. For the record, I do not personally discount these persons' knowledge. Folk medicine has been with us since the beginning of time.

Folk medicine carried on post-slavery out of tradition and necessity, due to a lack of access to formal healthcare because of a shortage of physicians, language or cultural barriers, poverty, or general mistrust of physicians (as was and still is the case with many black folk). Sadie's South Carolina upbringing was an example of home treatments as a result of lack of access.

SADIE GREEN

I was born in a house in Ridgeland, South Carolina. Wa'nt

no hospital when I was born. My granny delivered the babies. It was her and her sisters.

Having no hospitals or a shortage of black physicians (or white physicians who didn't mind tending to black patients) wasn't a concern in Savannah. Savannah has had black-owned and operated medical facilities and physicians for a very long time. Charity Hospital was owned and operated by power couple, Alice and Cornelius McKane. Georgia Infirmary was started by Thomas F. Williams, a white Savannah merchant and minister, who ordered its construction and chartered it in his last will and testament.

Alice Woodby McKane was the first black woman doctor in Savannah. She was born in 1865 in Pennsylvania, the same year the Confederates lost the Civil War and slavery ended legally. In 1882, she earned her medical degree from the Women's Medical College of Pennsylvania. She moved to Augusta, Georgia after graduating, becoming Georgia's first black woman licensed physician. (I make it a point to say licensed, because black women have been doctoring since the beginning of time.)

Alice was working in Augusta when she met Cornelius McKane, the grandson of a Liberian king. Cornelius was a surgeon, living in Savannah at the time. Alice moved to Savannah to join him, and together they built the first nurse training program for black folks in Southeast Georgia. After graduating four nurses, they moved to Liberia and made more history, opening Liberia's first hospital and nurse training school. The U.S. government appointed Alice as the medical examiner for black Civil War vets who moved from the U.S. to Liberia.

After Alice came down with the yellow fever, she and Cornelius moved back to Savannah. She opened a medical office on West Broad Street that specialized in gynecology and women's diseases. She petitioned Chatham County Superior

Court and got a charter to operate a hospital for women and children and a nursing school. That hospital, called McKane Hospital, opened in 1896.

In 1901, the hospital was adopted by a group of local black doctors and renamed Charity Hospital, where Ms. Florrie was born.

FLORRIE SCRIVEN

> My mom had three living children, because my brother, who was older than Lula Mae, he died at age two and was burned with pneumonia. Then she had three other kids stillborn. I was the only one born at Charity Hospital because when she became in labor, it was storming. So I was the only child that was born at Charity, because the doctors couldn't come to the house because of the weather. At Charity Hospital, that's where there were the black doctors, because that's where they went. Dr. Moore delivered me. He had his office on Montgomery Street. My goddaddy nicknamed me Stormy Weather. Anytime it storm, I'm in it.

Ms. Sadie actually worked for Charity in the 1940s and had a few memories of it, which were not all good.

SADIE GREEN

> I got a job working on Park Avenue to the children's home. They leave there and went to Greenbriar. Greenbriar was on Louisville Avenue. It got so big with so many children, they didn't have room so they had to build a place for them. They wanted me to go, but I wouldn't go. And after I leave there, I went to Charity Nursing Home. I was the cook there. I did everything there. When I got off from cooking, I would do

like maid work, see that the people was dressed proper, was clean or messed up. They paid me. I can't say I did it for nothing, but it wouldn't matter to me. But they had got so bad with the people.

I stopped working at Charity in '51. I told Dr. Milton—he worked at Charity too, but he had his office on West Broad Street. I told him about how bad the people was being treated. He said 'are you sho'? I said yeah, and we went down the cou'thouse. Dr. Milton and myself, we closed Charity.

The Georgia Infirmary was another medical facility and educational institution for black folk. In his final wishes, Thomas F. Williams wanted the hospital opened "for the relief and protection of afflicted and aged Africans" (Georgia Infirmary Historical Marker. 1910 Abercorn Street, Savannah, Georgia). Although it was not owned by black people, it served the black community. "It followed in the footsteps of the McKane Hospital for Women and Children and Training School for Nurses, which opened its doors to African Americans both seeking medical attention and desiring to enter the medical profession in the 1890s" (Georgia Historical Society).

FLORRIE SCRIVEN

Odell, my oldest girl, only girl, was born at Georgia Infirmary.

LULA MAE POLITE

I delivered my kids at Georgia Infirmary. Doctor C.E. Sax was my doctor and Dr. Harry Portman was my children's pediatrician. It was most white doctors in Georgia Infirmary, most were Jews. I saw him a good while ago. All them offices were right here on the east side between Abercorn and 34th. Dr. Sax and Dr. Portman they were right next to each other.

By far though, most black folk did not go to hospitals and doctors' offices. They handled everything in-home and mostly in conjunction with nature. African American folk medicine, in particular, combined African and Native American traditional medicine, creating what is known as "rootwork," since most of the medicines came from the roots of plants. The practice of rootwork, or folk medicine, is usually handed down from generation to generation by word of mouth.

CAROLYN DOWSE

> We didn't go to the doctor. Twice a year, you had to be cleaned out. Castor oil and orange juice. And I hated orange juice for the longest. If you got a cold, you put Camphor on your chest. We even took sugar and turpentine. My sister got all of that from her mother and her mother got it from her mother, and it was passed on. We did not go to doctors, and we were healthy.

More than 60 years younger than Ms. Dowse, I could relate to the castor oil clean out. In addition to the bi-annual dosage, I was also given the laxative anytime I got sick. According to the American Academy of Pediatrics News and Journals, "One tenet of the health belief system of black people is that illness is caused by "impurities" in the body and these impurities must be purged through the urine, the stool, or the skin (via rashes)....Other causes of illness in this health belief system include exposure to the elements (wind, cold, and rain), filth, improper diet, and irregular bowel movements."

Most folk remedies were salves, diuretics, or laxatives, which is where castor oil and cod liver oil (another one that I took as a child and gave to my own children) comes in.

RUBY JONES

We took castor oil for everything. Put it in something so it wouldn't taste so bad, but you still did. And all day when you belch, you tasted it. Used to grease yo insides. Everything come out. And cah'liv oil [cod liver oil]; it tastes fishy. And you know the toenail come off the pig? My father used to make something for colds. He put like whiskey in there and some other kind of medicine or something, and we would drink that. And he made a big jar and used to keep. I think it had red onions in it too.

SADIE GREEN

If somebody got cut, you put spiderweb and turpentine on it. Put a rag around it, 'cause it ain't been no Band-aids. If you got a cold, you take turpentine on sugar. After that, you get a bottle of castor oil.

CURT WILLIAMS

We didn't get sick often. Twice a year, we took yellow sulfur and honey, about a tablespoon. We also took worm medicine with a lemon wedge and a peppermint stick. Then we had something that I take to this day. It's called rabbit tobacco, and it only grows in the cemetery. Get that and you can either steep it for tea or roll it up and smoke it. All I know is that they say it make you live a long time.

MARY BUTLER SMITH

My grandfather, who was full blood Cherokee Indian, used to take brown liquor, onion, honey, and lemon. Boil all that together and give it to us whenever we got sick. He called it tea. It would knock you out and you'd sweat something serious in your sleep. By the time you wake up, you'd be good as new.

Then there's a side of rootwork used to enhance or disrupt a person's life with the use of herbs, minerals, bodily fluids, personal possessions, and even animal parts, along with supernatural forces. As many recipes that exist to remedy certain ailments, there are just as many that are conjured to either harm people physically or spiritually, or to emotionally manipulate them (i.e. make your husband disinterested in his mistress). Another word for this practice is hoodoo.

For the record, there is a huge difference between hoodoo and voodoo, terms that are often wrongly used interchangeably. Both are spiritual practices that originate in West Africa but voodoo and hoodoo exist for different purposes. Voodoo (also known as voudon) means "spirit" and is a religion with its own set of leaders, dogmas, services, and rituals. Loas—a family of spirits—are worshipped and called on during rituals. Like saints in Catholicism, each loa has its own association and representation.

Ms. Sadie Green's story below represents the kind of rootwork that you may better recognize as hoodoo, folk magic, dark magic, hexing, or roots and conjure. This kind was intended to harm, not heal.

SADIE GREEN

Roots and conjure, that's true. I'm a living witness. That's real. Don't let nobody tell you it's not real. I don't know what they do, but I know they can do it. I went through that with my aunt and another lady with a clothesline in Bloomingdale. They used to use [noose] the clothes line together. My aunt had the clothes on the line, and this lady wanted to put her clothes on that side of the line. I remember the lady said, no because I'll take the line down. She said if you take it down, you won't remember putting it back up. She said I'm going in my house. Just like that. The lady went in her house. My aunt went in her house. The lady come back. I said to my aunt, that lady putting powder under the line. She said, powder? I say, yeah. She say, just like that, that bitch ain't putting no powder down there. That bitch tryna root me. My uncle say, y'all need to stop that foolishness.

My aunt went and put the clothes on the line. When she hang up the first piece, she fall on the second piece. She fall on the second piece she got to hang up. She did not listen. We tell her not to walk because that lady had sprinkled powder down there. And she walked anyhow. She walked one-sided from then until she went to God. That leg drawed up. Like how people having one leg longer than the other. That's how her leg was. And that was over day. She didn't hang up the second piece.

But me and her daughter, we had sense enough to know it ain't no powder had no business sprinkling under no line. And we told her mama, and she say, that ain't no powder. That bitch don' poisoned my daughter, just like that. We say, we told yo daughter not to go there. She was in her do' looking and then my aunt closed her do. She wanted to see if it was gon' work or if that lady did it for show, but it worked.

RUBY JONES

> It was a lot of roots going on. They used to say they brought it over from Carolina, but I wasn't into that. I didn't believe it. I guess people could hurt you. I just didn't believe you could just put something on somebody and hurt 'em, but maybe if you eat something or drink something, it could hurt you.

As with most cultural practices directly derived from Africa, you're seen as slow, country, or backwards for taking part in it. It's not only shamed but sometimes dismissed. Regarding hoodoo and rootwork in general, non-believers often dismiss it as useless nonsense or they believe that it works but only if you believe in it (as is the case of Ms. Ruby). One thing that cannot be denied, however: the positions of power it put its practitioners in—especially back in the day.

"[A]lthough command of this lore led to women and people of color being labeled as 'backward,' 'ignorant,' and 'superstitious' by educated white men, their occult knowledge gave them the ability to manipulate the social world and improve their status within it" (Kordas, 2016). This was the case with Marie Laveau in New Orleans, for example, and Dr. Buzzard, a South Carolina native who traveled the low country for his hoodoo work and who's been referenced in countless writings.

RECREATION

Roots had yet another purpose too: fun! Ms. Madie shared something that she did with roots that I would've never thought of (and still can't quite picture).

MADIE UNDERWOOD

> I loved doll babies, which I never had a doll until I was about eight or nine years old before I had a doll. You know what we used to have for a doll baby? We pulled the grass up, and the roots of the grass was the doll's hair. We'd get a piece of string and tie it 'round the top part and that would be the doll itself. And you'd tie a little string about halfway around the doll and then we'd wash it. Wash all the dirt out the roots and that would be the doll's hair. And we was so happy. What we had to play with was bugs and insects. That was our toys. That's the God honest truth. I lived that. That was my childhood life.

A common misconception about the time period of 1920 through 1970 for black folk is that their lives were consumed with the bad. That was definitely my assumption on it during grade school years. From the tragedies of slavery to the humiliations of Jim Crow, I couldn't imagine how anyone could experience any semblance of joy through any of that. But that's simply not the truth. Regardless of what any oppressed people go through, they will always find a reason to smile—if even for just a second. Black Savannah had plenty of good times, as children, as teenagers, and later as adults.

FLORRIE SCRIVEN

I never did like the house. I was the one that was always gone. Gone, gone, gone, to this day. "You know Mama gon' whip you. Why you keep going? You know you gon' get a whipping," they'd say. "Well, I'll just get it when I get back." I'd be right over there in Yamacraw Village playing, trying to learn how to ride bicycles and all that kind of stuff and skate. One of my schoolmates, they lived in Yamacraw Village. We were in Indian Lane. And so after school, instead of me coming home, I would go to their house and try to ride the bicycle and skate and mess my clothes up. I to' up my clothes and fell all in the bushes, the hedges, and get all scratched up and everything. I was strictly a tomgirl.

LULA MAE POLITE

My daddy went to church with us. There was a time he had drop out, but he went back. My mama she never sent us to church. All us went together. Not one time could we go and leave her home. My daddy had the key to the church, and sometimes he'd give us the key. I was so angry when he'd give us that key 'cause we had to be there to open up.

Down there through that subway on West Boundary,

you could go down through that and get to Jones, and we was right at the church. My mama would say don't y'all go through that subway and I'd say no ma'am we ain't going. We would leave early, don't y'all go through that subway now and y'all better be there when I get there. Yes ma'am. My aunt lived in Garrard Lane, that was right there off Oglethorpe Street. And she had a lot of children, but they didn't go to church. And we would stop by there and play a while and then we would look at that clock and we'd take off. Mama get to church and we'd been don' sit down and try to keep from blowing hard, be so tired.

RUBY JONES

For fun, we rode bikes. We played hopscotch, jump rope, and different things. Then in May when they have May festivals, we all get dressed up pretty and have May festival at the school. If the chil'ren today could only know.

STEVEN WILLIAMS

We would crowd around, stand on the corner and talk. As far as having possession of things, we didn't have nothing. We made our own scooters. You take a piece of board, usually an ole' two by four or something like that, attach the skates to the board, and take another two by four and hook it onto that to make the handle. We made our own toys. Only thing you could really rely on at Christmas time, and everybody had the same thing: a pair of skates and a cap pistol. That's about it. It was a struggle, but at the same time, we still had a lot of fun.

SADIE GREEN

We used to go play basketball on Saturdays. Jump rope, hopscotch. We did all of that.

CAROLYN DOWSE

We didn't have a car, so on Sunday afternoons, we would get on the Mill Haven bus and ride all the way to the end of the line then pay another fare. We made our recreation, you know?

MARY BUTLER SMITH

There were times when Dad would come home and drive up and blow the horn and we knew we were going for a ride. We'd go racing to the car and Mama would come out and get in the back seat. He said, "Come on, Queen. Get in the back with me." And she said, "I'm tired. I don't feel like driving." And he said, "No, Mamie has been bugging me to let her drive. She told me she know how to drive." I got in the front seat and I had been standing up behind him for the longest time looking over his shoulder seeing how the gears shift. I didn't ask to be taught, I just asked to drive. He got tired of hearing it, so on this night, he didn't offer any assistance. He just said, you said you could drive and I'll give you the chance to drive.

The block we lived in, the 900-block was slight incline, but it was going down a little bit. I got in the car and turned the ignition on and put the gear where it was supposed to go and started off down the street, slowly. Got down to the corner, made a left turn, and two blocks over was Victory

Drive. Got there, made a left turn again, drove down another block to where I'd make another left turn to come back to the house. Got back home safe. Stopped the car, put it in gear, turned off the ignition. "How did I do, Daddy?" "You did well," he said. "But you won't get behind the wheel of any car of mine until I say so. Don't ask me." I didn't drive it again until I was up in my teens.

FLORRIE SCRIVEN

Walking was transportation from the east side to the west side. Now the girls could do that, but not the boys, because there was a separating line. Bull Street was the separating line from the east to the west. The west side boys didn't allow the east side boys to come over and get the girls. I had a east side and a west side boyfriend though. Most of the young men were afraid of my dad. There was one young man, he lived right in the community on Indian Street. We lived in Indian Lane. He liked me so much, and I liked him too. He wanted to take me to the prom, but he was so afraid of my dad. So I think he went around to the back door instead of the front door. And then after that, I met my daughter's dad, and my son's, both kids have the same dad. His mom had a lil sto' down on Zubler and Fahm, they used to call the Pablo Store. Piccolo, we used to gather there to dance and have a lot of fun there. He and I, yeah, we got together.

They used to call us the Technicolor Girls, the three of us. We had our ballerina shoes, and we would color them. Whatever we were wearing, the ballerinas would be that same color.

ROOSEVELT ROUSE

I didn't know no girls and nothing but a few boys when I first moved to Savannah. I knew some young guys lived down the street from me. They daddy had a car that he seldom drove, so we used to get in that car and we used to ride all over Savannah, Carolina, and stuff like that. Lymus Middleton. He used to let them boys have that car and we'd get in that car and ride and ride and ride and ride. The only thing he used to ask was, don't bring my car home with no gas in it. That was it.

It was gangs here during that time when I was coming up. I wasn't gon' get in no gang, but I wa'nt gon' let no gang mess with me either and that's why I stayed away. I had a few friends. They used to come to my house or I went to they house. But nothing like go stand out on the corner or no shit like that. Walk down there on Augusta Avenue, there was always a bunch of people out there. I walked up there on August Avenue and I jumped up on one of them tall white post with the name of the street on it. I was sitting up on one. I can't think of them boys last name, it was three of 'em, and one of 'em come up. I was sitting up on the post and he come mess with me, mess with me. I said, "Why don't you gon' leave me alone? I'm not bothering you." He said, "I'm gon' pull you down off that pole and whip you." He pulled me down and I came down swinging. I knocked his ass out.

I didn't knock him out, but when he got up, he hauled ass. His older brother was right 'cross the street. I was late teens, I'd say. He became my best friend after that and stayed my best friend 'til I become married. I caught some hell in my day, but I had some good times too.

Mr. Johnnie had his own bully-turned-friend story.

JOHNNIE PARRISH

Mama kept us clean even though you ain't had nothing but a pair of overalls and a pair of dress clothes. Well, you had two pair of overalls. One you shoot marbles in and the other you kept it for to go to school. 'Cause even though my mama had all them boys, we all wore overalls. My grandmama was a seamstress and she didn't go to school to learn her trade, but she made all her grandchildren clothes. With WWII, you couldn't get no blue denim, but you could get that striped mattress tick[ing] cloth.

People used to see us coming, they say, "Well y'all better step aside 'cause here come them lil chain gang boys" 'cause we had on them striped overalls. But we didn't bother people. You know how they beat up people children now? We didn't play that when we was coming up. What the big boys used to do. You see a boy picking on a boy or bullying a boy, first thing you find out what grade he in. He in my grade, they tell me, "go get him, Sunny." So I'll go up, "Man, what you picking on that lil boy? You wanna fight somebody, fight me!" And the big boy'll stand back because he know your brother ain't gon' let you get beat up. I always wanted to be like a cowboy like Johnnie Mac Brown. I'd hit 'em up and knock 'em out. Then that same boy you fought, he become to be yo friend.

MARY BUTLER SMITH

The church used to have, not parties, but cookouts in our backyard. Daddy would string lights back there and dig a pit in the ground and they would roast barbecue. The whole neighborhood would smell good. And mama and the other ladies would make the potato salad and other stuff to go along with it. And we had a ball, I'm telling you. Good times, good times. Good clean fun. And we used to do...they had a party boat on the river that you could rent and I don't know whether it was black-owned or whatever, but we could afford it. Our church. We would rent that boat and go for a ride and have all kinds of food and music and entertainment and dancing. We'd just have a good time. Yes, indeed. We had to make our own pastimes. You had to, back then, find a way to do what you wanted to do.

FLORRIE SCRIVEN

As I got older, I used to go on the boat to have fun too. Now that's where the devil crabs and shrimps and the red rice and all that good stuff was over there. Those women would be selling, you know? We'd dock the boat on River Street. Captain Sam owned that boat, and they made sure they took it from him. Some kind of oil mess. Took that boat from him. That was a source of pride for us too. You could rent it out. We had so much fun going to St. Helena Island and Daufuskie Island. That's where it went at and docked and we got off and those people were out there, you know, with the crabs and devil crabs and shrimp. Oh wow, that was the life.

CURT WILLIAMS

We had the Dirtsons, Gunnie Greene, Spokema Park, Coconut Grove, one mo club that sit up there where Planet Fitness at now owned by black, and The Flamingo. The Flamingo, the only big entertainment club in Savannah we had, where all the big stars--Aretha Franklin and James Brown--that's where the new civic center gon' be at. They gon' make parking out of that. The man that ownded all that property, his name was William J. Belgium. Oh, that was a big man. And his wife was uneducated. White man came. We don't have that no mo. Everytime I pass through that area, 'cause my sister still got the big house that we grew up in out there, I look at all that property.

Then we had a Black Diamond where all the black teens come out and play baseball. The city closed it down. Because we made money back in them days. They closed it down and then they put everything out there on Eisenhower. All the stadiums, we got to go out there on Eisenhower. And the one we had out there on President Street, there was a black one out there on President Street. Now look how they letting Eisenhower run down. Look at the concession stands. Only thing they keeping up halfway right is the soccer field 'cause all of dem play soccer.

FLORRIE SCRIVEN

My friend who was my boyfriend's sister, Dorothy and Thelma, well we didn't do the local clubs here. We went out with the elites. Gunnie Greene, he had a club out in Tremont Park, so that's where we went on Sunday night. The school teachers and the upper echelon. It was my pastor's wife's sister's husband's place.

I also organized a group called the Melonettes. We were inducted into the Gospel Music Hall of Fame. We're in the museum. I named the group for the voice, the mellow voice, the melodious voice.

SADIE GREEN

We party, house parties. We was too busy selling food to go to a club, but we would gamble all night at the house parties.

Shooting dice and everything else. We have had parties from Friday to Monday morning. It was good parties.

Fun for black folk back then was not only natural, but it was a form of resistance. If we think about all the discriminatory milestones they lived through on top of all the chores they were given, to still have it in them to let it all go and have fun is amazing. Fun was necessary to balance out the dense responsibilities, and there were many.

CHAPTER FOUR

GETTING GROWN

"I was a hustler all my life." -Sadie Green

Many of the elders started working at a young age. When I say "work" here, I mean entering the workforce where income was made in some capacity outside of chores or in-house responsibilities. In many cases, it was out of necessity. Their parents and guardians needed more income, so their children would be required to not only work but share their earnings. That was the case for Ms. Madie. Even when she got married, she still gave her Mom half of what she made.

Going to work, I realized, was something like a rite of passage for today's elders. Entering the workforce seemed to mark the transition from childhood to adulthood. 1 Corinthians 13:11, a scripture that I seemed to remember from the first time I heard it, reads, "When I was a child, I spoke as a child, I understood as a child, I thought as a child; but when I became a man, I put away childish things." From my personal experience of going to work at the age of 14, I can say for certain that once I started working, I, too, put childish things away.

Back on the coasts of West Africa, our ancestors celebrated the transition into adulthood in ways that varied from community to community. Rites of passages were lifelong events. Unique communal celebrations were in place for birth, puberty, marriage, and death. Though the type of ritual varied, the unifying force was community. The whole village—the family and the neighborhood—came together to acknowledge the individual's transition.

With the loss of the rites of passage, evolving into adulthood also lost its custom of calling you by your name, praising your contributions to society, and welcoming you into the next phase of your life. Putting away childish things usually stemmed from going out into the world and making money.

WORKING AS CHILDREN

For most, gaining employment happened around the age of 13 or 14. For some, as in the case of Ms. Madie and Ms. Sadie, working outside of the home happened as early as eight years old.

MADIE UNDERWOOD

> We were well-trained. We trained with responsibility. So I started working, earning some money to help when I was eight years old. I was babysitting. And I was babysitting for a white nurse, and it look like to me she'd have better sense than to leave her baby with an eight year old kid, you know? I knew how to take care of a baby sometimes better than some of these grown women do. They trained me when I was little how to change those babies, keep them clean, keep 'em fed, keep 'em burped, teach 'em how to walk, show 'em how to play, teach 'em how to talk. They taught us that at very young ages.
>
> The lady she would call me. She had a phone. We didn't have no phone at home, but she had one and she would call

me and tell me different things to do for the baby. She had a rocking chair, and I was really excited about that.

I had a job working when I was eight years old taking care of babies. I always look back at that and say they just didn't wanna pay money. And as long as you can do the job, that's all that mattered, and I could do the job. I kept that baby clean, I kept that baby fed, I did the job. I was getting paid fifty cents a day for five days a week from 8 to 5, during the summer when I was out of school. Mama never demanded our money. She always let us give her what we wanted to give her, and so I'd always give Mom half of what I made. Even when I got married and worked, I would still give Mom half of what I made.

Now when I was about 11, I was working at places like restaurants and hotels. After school jobs and during summer vacations. My mama wanted us to go to school no matter what. That was very important to her. Now my dad was different. My dad said if you can read and you can count, get yourself a job. When I would leave school, I would go to work. When I would leave work, I still had chores to do when I came home. Everybody had an assignment. Then I'd get my schoolwork done and wash my one pair of socks. I mostly washed my socks when I first came home because I only had one pair until I got in high school. I think I had two pair when I got in high school. We had one pair of shoes, two pair of socks, and we had ribbons and barrettes and stuff to put on your hair. Mom made her own soap.

I never knew how she made it. She never taught us that thing. The soap mama made was for laundry, shampoo, baths, cleaning, and everything. I know she used lye and white potatoes. Whatever else she used, I don't know. We had what you call a big iron wash pot in the backyard, and she would make the soap in there. That's also where we'd wash our clothes by hand, and they had to be rinsed three times, and then hung on lines to dry.

Ms. Sadie offered a little more information on her cleaning and cleanser-making process.

SADIE GREEN

> Wash your clothes in a tub and boil your clothes in the pot, so it'll be clean. I did that too. Wasn't no Clorox. We used potash to clean the clothes.

Again, our elders were minimalists way before that was even a word. It was just the passed down lifestyle. Just as Ms. Madie's mama used that one soap for nearly all of her cleaning purposes, the pot was multi-functional as well.

MADIE UNDERWOOD

> In that same wash pot, my daddy was a fisherman and a hunter. When he would go fishing, he would bring back burlap bags from anywhere from fifty to hundred pound size full of crabs, shrimp, oysters, fish. He would bring back all kinds of stuff like that. Because you know Savannah is the largest seaport city in the South.

Fishing and hunting were common. We were a very self-reliant people, not just depending on the grocery store or butcher to provide our meals. We independently gathered our own goods to keep our families whole and well. Sisters Florrie and Lula Mae shared their memories on that subject too.

FLORRIE SCRIVEN

> My dad would go fishing and hunting, and he would bring

back those things—coons and all of that. Lula Mae can tell you a lot of about that, because she was more homely than I was.

LULA MAE POLITE

We kept fish, coon, and alligator tail in the house. I can recall a time when I liked to cook. Daddy liked to cook too. My mama didn't do much cooking at home. If my daddy felt like at two o'clock in the morning eating something, he would get up and start cooking and I'd be right there with him. Me and him would always be cooking something.

Chores had a lot to do with eating too. When fathers would go off hunting and fishing, someone had to clean the fresh catches of the day. That responsibility, as well as cooking, would oftentimes fall into the lap of the children of the house. By far, though, chores consisted of keeping house (and helping Mama keep other folks' houses).

MADIE UNDERWOOD

As we got bigger, Mama would take housework and she would take in people's laundry. People used to bring they laundry to the house and we had to wash all that stuff by hand, dry it on a line in the yard, and then iron it with a smoothing iron. Not an electric iron. An iron that you had to heat on a coal pot in a fireplace. That's the way we made a living during that time. So the kids were taught responsibility at a very young age. And they worked at a very young age to try to get ahead. That's why I was so interested in my children getting an education so they wouldn't have to go through that kind of junk. But through all of that, we lived.

Ms. Sadie also worked since she was eight years old, and although those years of her life were spent in South Carolina, I wanted to include them to show a similarity between rural life and urban life. Regardless if you lived in the country or the city, going to work at a young age was something you had to do.

SADIE GREEN

I was working since I was eight years old. I was always going in the white folks' house. I used to go and like live-in. I used to keep my great-grandmama Hannah too. She didn't want nobody to keep her but me. On Fridays, my great-aunt was home and I could go to school. I went to school every Friday. Kids went when they could back then. We used to walk to school from the plantation.

JOHNNIE PARRISH

Soon as you got 18, they classed you 1A in a few weeks you was gone whether you attended school or not. My older brother after he finish school was drafted in World War II. During that time when they started drafting, they knew we was hard workers. They told us Uncle Sam wanted some good men. So when they tell you 'good men,' a black man was first being a 'good man.' So if it was a war going on, we didn't have to go in the service. The boss man got to keep us out like he kept his children out. But that depend on what kind of boss man you had. A good boss man was based on what kind of sharecropper he had, you see? If you made the boss man money—and we made all them white people rich, we did, black folks—we didn't have to go in the service 'lessen we wanted to.

STEVEN WILLIAMS

After high school, I got in the Air Force. I volunteered. The service was a lifesaver for black boys. That was the place to go. That was one of the best decisions I'd ever made when I went in the service. What they called it then was OJT, on-the-job training. It simply meaned whatever they gave you to do, you did. It was quite an adventure going in the Air Force as an eighteen year old black boy.

LULA MAE POLITE

When I was in high school, I worked when school was out. My aunt worked at Savoy Cafe. It was on Whitaker and Congress Lane. When school was out, she would get me a job. I would go up there and get a job washing dishes. I didn't get paid that much, about $12 for a week. $12.50. That was a lot of money. I'd give my mama half.
    Another thing we used to do, we used to sell on the street. You know butterbeans. We used to shell the butterbeans and we would go in the white people neighborhood and say, "Butterbeans, green peas." And they would come to the do' and call you and buy it. That's what I did.

CURT WILLIAMS

When I was lil boy, I used to throw papers for the Savannah Morning News on bicycle.

FLORRIE SCRIVEN

I worked at the Kessler's restaurant with my mom and aunts

for a little while, but it wasn't for me. It was one Saturday morning and business was kind of slow. He says, "Well maybe Florrie, you can clean the windows." I said, "No, I don't think so. I'll tell you what. I'll just go home." And I walked from the farmer's market, in what's now City Market, to Traffic Circle, out 80 West, and caught the bus and came home. I was maybe about 15.

LULA MAE POLITE

I got my first real job at Morrison Cafeteria. Morrison used to be right at the corner of Congress and Whitaker. I was a maid. We used to work in the dining room, cleaning the tables off for the waiters. Do the tables. Then I worked at Tradewinds. That's where I got all those people enrolled with the SCLC. It was a shrimp factory in Thunderbolt. If you ever go to a seafood place out there near Mall Blvd, Fiddler's, they got all of the old pictures of Tradewinds in there.

ROOSEVELT ROUSE

I had to stop school in third grade, but I was still able to get pretty good jobs. Like I said, I came to Savannah when I was

14. I stayed with my Aunt Wesley Lee Davis, my mother's sister. She was a Gaines 'til she got married. I got a job here 'cause her husband worked there. It was called Pellpoint. Pellpoint Box Factory. I went there for about two years and they shut that down. After that, I went to a fertilizer mill. It was out there on Lathrop Ave, then they shut down. They always was shut down a certain time of year, though, because nobody was planting.

Anyway when I left there, I went to the inspection company. Reason I left there 'cause they was, they um, they let one guy go on vacation and it wasn't nothing but three of us working together, in the shipping department, in the trucks. They let the cake loader go and told us we had to do it all. I said not me. I ain't gon' do no 2-man work with the same pay. I asked him. I say, "you gon' pay me more?" he said no. I said, "You better get somebody else." Wa'nt nobody working in the shipping department, but one white dude.

When I left, I was walking 'cause I didn't have a car. I still wasn't nothing but 'bout 15 or 16 years old. I heard the car blowing and blowing, so he stopped. He quit too. He followed me and took me over to the bus stop 'cause I was catching the bus, going back home. One day I came home and saw my old bossman truck outside, from Derst Baking Company truck. He come to try to get me to go back. He said you a good worker. You the best worker we got. He said why don't you come on back. I said no. He wasn't the one I got in the argument with now.

WORKING AS AN ADULT

ROOSEVELT ROUSE

Left from [Derst] and the next job I had was at Great Dane Trailer. I stayed there 23 years...Then I went to work at Georgia Pacific, then I went to work for the city 'til I retired.

SADIE GREEN

We used to go out there and sell bolitas, the numbers. We had something like a book, and the book it would go back. So like you got 10 pages of 1 to 100, and if you want the 5, 1 or the 5, 10, or the 5 or whatever, then you take and tear that off and give it to them. You had 100 leafs in that book. If it come out, they got it on that paper. Bring that paper to you and whatever it's worth, then you pay 'em.

Oh, I made all kinds of money in this man's town. I thought it was mine one time. You'd win at least a dollar. We made our own numbers from 1 to 100. Now it's the Cash Three. It was Joe Louis, they was the head, and we worked under them. They told us what the winning number was, and we told the people.

Anytime you can sell bolita, and I'm saying it 'cause it's true, then you can make $500 a week, sometimes a day. We never went by ourselves. We used to have our basket. You know how they have the baskets on they head? I never was a head basket. I used to put mine in my hand. But we had fun. We sold bolita, whiskey, food. Savannah don't owe me nothing.

STEVEN WILLIAMS

After working in the industry as a casual worker and making my hours, I was given the honor and privilege of becoming a member of this great UNION. For a man who came to this place as a drunken bum with no profession and very much unskilled, this UNION was my finest hour.

After I regularly began attending the membership meetings, I was introduced to the labor movement and union politics by the Recording Secretary at the time, Mr. John H. Mackey. In 1977 the membership blessed me by electing me to the position of Recording Secretary for the Union. I served in this position for twelve (12) uninterrupted years and those were the best years of my life. Serving in the capacity of Recording Secretary gave me the opportunity to travel to many great countries at home and abroad. I have visited Canada and I have mixed with and broke bread with the greatest political and labor leaders in this country. Without a doubt, the greatest honor of my life has been for me to have served this UNION to the best of my capabilities as Recording Secretary…

FLORRIE SCRIVEN

I went to American Baptist in Nashville, Tennessee and I went to Howard University and Georgia State in Atlanta. I did my practical at Georgia State for first and second offenders.

I met my friend after I went there because I wanted to do jail counseling and so we did GEDs and simple math and English and all that for them. Several of them went to the college from there. That was quite an experience. Next door, we had the work study. So they'd come there and go to work. Back in what they called the halfway house. It was like a rehabilitation center.

I went on East Broad Street when they first opened that place on East Broad Street and I was applying there and he was asking, "What you plan to do if you're hired here?" I said, "Well, I plan to work with the inmates and try to get them rehabilitated." He said, "We're not here for that." I was so shocked. They're just getting money. It's a lucrative business.

CURT WILLIAMS

I used to work for Georgia Regional for 14 years for special needs students. I liked that job. I worked to Georgia Regional, I was a cook for the Pirate House for 14 years. I worked to the Coca Cola bottling company. We used to make Coke right there on East Broad and Bay Street. That was the Coca Cola company there. I was a inspector because the white man said, "Boy, I like yo work." I never was a man now. He had one black guy--we only had one black guy knew the formula to make coke, and we made it with real cocaine. You didn't know that, did you? We had to dump big bags over in a big ole' pot and it was pure cocaine. You ever tried to taste a real Coke Cola back then and drink it, it'll burn your throat. Back then, we wa'nt allowed to buy Coke. A lot of people didn't know that. You could only buy orange sodas and grape sodas. They would not serve a black man a Coke Cola. I'll never forget, the sto' is still out there on Louisville Road. It's closed down, but the building is still there. Steve's Corner, it's called, it's still out there.

I'd heard that Coca Cola used cocaine as one of its secret ingredients before, but I had never heard that black men were not allowed to purchase Coca Cola. In a *New York Times* op-ed entitled "When Jim Crow Drank Coke," Grace Elizabeth Hale, history and American studies professor at University of Virginia, supported everything Curt said—from the addition of cocaine to the soft drink to possible reasons why black men were not allowed to purchase the drink. "Middle-class whites worried that soft drinks were contributing to what they saw as exploding cocaine use among African-Americans. Southern newspapers reported that "negro cocaine fiends" were raping white women, the police powerless to stop them" (2013). Coca Cola disputed this information on their website.

Coca Cola was the last job that Curt held.

CURT WILLIAMS

When I was lil boy, I used to throw papers for the Savannah Morning News on bicycle. Then it was Georgia Regional, the Pirate House, the Coca Cola bottling company. I say when I get 35, I say I ain't gon' work for nobody but myself, and I hit it on the head and never looked back. You got to have a drive, and you make a decision on what you gonna do in life, and do it.

For most men coming up, Mr. Curt Williams and Mr. Steven Williams included, military service was the next step after your eighteenth birthday.

JOHNNIE PARRISH

Soon as you got 18, they classed you 1A in a few weeks you was gone whether you attended school or not. All us was good men, you know hard-working guys, clean cut guys.

These young men who were drafted in the military were sent to war: World War II, the Korean War, or the Vietnam War. War veterans often come home with seen and unseen wounds that inevitably affect their loved ones as well. Ms. Mary Smith's story is a testament of that.

MARY BUTLER SMITH

I got pregnant before I knew anything about getting pregnant. When I got married, soon after that, I was pregnant. I thought it was a way of escape, a way of getting out, but it was like going from bad to worse.

The man I married was a service man and he went overseas after we married, and he left me with the baby. When he came back, he was less of a man than when he went over there. He made the mistake of striking me. I didn't tell my daddy 'cause he would've shot him and I know it. But I did tell my daddy that I wanted to go up north.

In the course of "getting grown," stories of starting a family were also discussed.

STARTING FAMILIES

MARY BUTLER SMITH

I broke away from my second husband too. I don't let nobody abuse me. This second husband, he made the mistake of putting his hand on me. He hit me across my face, across my lip. I remember splitting my lip. When I insisted that I was going to the doctor, he took me to the doctor, and waited on me and acted like a colored gentleman supposed to act. But I wasn't having any of it. That was the end of that.

I was living, then, in Philadelphia with this husband who worshipped the ground I walked on. He used to live back on 41st Street, in the second house from the corner. That corner is bare now. There was a home out there. One of my good friends, her husband was a barber and the lady and my mama was really good friends. The lady had a brother who lived in Philadelphia. He came down to visit his sister and met me. At that time, we used to entertain servicemen at different churches and whatnot.

Smitty came down and he met me and almost didn't want to go back to Philadelphia. I drove back to Philly with him in his car. He was so insistent. He was a mixed breed--jolly, stout, good-looking, yellow man. I say yellow man, light brown skinned, I guess. He just fell for me. He had a beautiful house in Philadelphia on West 57th Street in a row house in a mainly black neighborhood. Fine homes. But row houses, I wasn't familiar with that at all. I thought that was like for po' folks, you know what I'm saying? I was used to homes, you see.

He wanted me to move in and I said not without marrying me. He said, whatever it takes, baby. And so we married, making him my third husband, and I moved in. Whatever I wanted, he got. My daddy bought me a piano after I told him I wanna learn how to play the piano like Frieda, that was our church pianist and she taught music. I was taking music so I could practice my lessons at home. In a week or two, the piano was sitting up in the house. Smitty bought my second piano to entice me to come live in Philadelphia with him. He wasn't the ideal husband, but he treated me well and I treated him well.

FLORRIE SCRIVEN

Your body opens up once you've delivered your baby, so you need to put everything back in shape. Take that sheet and wrap it around you tight. Pull your body back together. That's healthy. And you did not go outside for a span of 30 days, a month. Couldn't even go to the kitchen. Because they say, you know, you were nasty. You couldn't do no cooking or nothing like that. Couldn't wash your hair, take a shower, none of that. No.

LULA MAE POLITE

When my daughter was a baby, I moved out. They told me I couldn't take her with me. If you wanna go, get yo clothes and go, but Lynn stays. I can see her right now, sitting--the sofa was right by the do' and she was sitting on the sofa. And my daddy said you go. I was tryna put the drop on my mama. She wasn't there. My mama wasn't there when I went there, just my daddy. My daddy say young lady, you wanna go, go 'head but Lynn stays.

So all of our children called us by our name and our mama Mama and our daddy Daddy. And that's the way, you know like, I see now, if you raising children and you don't say take this and give it to your daddy, they'll raise up saying Daddy. All of my children raise up calling Arthur, Arthur. Now the boys, the boys they call 'em Pop. Shaquita, my youngest daughter, she the only one call him Daddy. The rest of 'em say Arthur. And I'm Lula Mae. They kinda cut it short, they say Normy.

JOHNNIE PARRISH

Back then, you couldn't put your hands on girls during that time. Guy go and put his arm around a girl, a girl'll knock yo.... Girls wasn't nothing like they is now. We had to be 18 years old before we could really court—go see a girl. Then you could put your hand on her. Most times you put your hand on her when her mama and yo mama felt like well that's his high school sweetheart and they gon' get married, then you could ease your hand around her arm. This my high school sweetheart. During that time, being young, my mama taught us, if you impregnate somebody daughter, you married her. That's why, you ever heard somebody talk about the shotgun wedding?

DOROTHY PARRISH

I came to Savannah in 58. That was our wedding day and we left Swainsboro, which is Emmanuel County. We roomed in the house with three people until we had our first child and we only had use of the bathroom, the kitchen, and our private bedroom. Then we would go to church. Our church was on 48th and MLK. We would go to church. We was one of the few churches at that time that had church on Sunday nights, and our young folk would also have what they called BYPU in the evening and then we would have church at night. Our church was a very small church and our children would be so many that at the end of the vocation bible school, we would go on a trip, Carowinds, Brunswick, and Six Flags. We used to take two Greyhound buses. Children on one bus and grown people on the other. We started doing that in the 60s. We did good in this town 'cause we had our life together when we met.

CHAPTER FIVE

COMMUNITIES AND CORRIDORS

"We stuck together." -Florrie Scriven

Beginning in Africa and extending through slavery, freedom, Reconstruction, the Great Depression, Jim Crow, and the Great Migration, black folks lived by the old saying "We all we got." That's not to say that the community didn't have its fair share of Uncle Toms or nose-in-the-air, only-care-for-self individuals. But larger than that was the camaraderie—within family, the neighborhood, the school, the church, etc. There was a village approach to nearly every facet of life. Whether you were well-to-do or dirt poor, a strong sense of community was a constant.

SADIE GREEN

Everybody had kids and we took care of our kids. If one didn't have enough money to buy food for that child, we did it. She would give it back when she get it, when she have her gain, she would give it back. Sometimes it leave her completely broke with nothing. But her light, her water, and her rent, we see that that was paid. Ain't been no pampers, but diapers. See that she kept them diapers clean. I used to run the business then too. I give them many diapers. I didn't regret it then and if I had to do it all over, I wouldn't regret it now.

MADIE UNDERWOOD

We moved to West Savannah on Cope Street with my Aunt Eva and Uncle Bubba and they had two children of their own 'cause my Uncle Buddy had been married before. His wife had passed away, so he had two children and my Aunt Eva helped him finish raising his children. Later on, she had another child, but when we moved in with them, they only had the two children. Now they had their own home, but they only had two bedrooms, a living room, kitchen, a big backyard. So there was ten people coming to live with them who was desperate, no food, no money, no clothes, no nothing but a big problem. But they took our family in.

Then my Uncle Buddy was working on the railroad and Eva was keeping house, so they made a deal. He would say, well she would go out and go to work. Mama stayed home to keep her children and Aunt Eva's two, so that's how she got ten kids. And Dad and Uncle Buddy...and in that time and even when I left Savannah, a job was still easy to find. Even when I moved to Philly, jobs was easy to find. You wanna work, you just go out and get yourself a job. That's the way it was at that time. So this is the way we got started in Savannah. So Daddy got a job and as soon as he made a couple pays, he was able to get him a place to stay with his family and start from there. That was in West Savannah on Norton Street.

Neighborhood was just like family. Anybody had a problem, everybody had a problem. Everybody looked out for each other. And most of us helped each other. You know like one was less fortunate, I was a part of that group, I mean people would always be doing things for us. My daddy was a fisherman and a hunter, and when he used to go out when he go fishing, he would bring crabs by the 50-sack. He had what they called croaker sacks during that time. Daddy would bring those big bags of crab home. He'd bring the big bags of shrimp, and he would just pass it out to the whole neighborhood.

Steven Williams, a Savannah native, also experienced poverty growing up. Yet, like Madie, he could still count on his people to be there for him.

STEVEN WILLIAMS

Some people that had it good, whose parents had good jobs, they didn't act that head on the shoulders. They was with us. We was all together. There was no big me, little you.

CAROLYN DOWSE

I was born in 741 East Anderson. The house is no longer there, they demolished it. My sister ended up, when she first got married, she bought a house on Bolton Street, and in the city, this was not Sapelo, but in the city, we had the outdo' toilet. This was Savannah. A lot of people thought that was only in the country. And we took a bath once a week in a tin tub, her husband, everybody, in a tin tub, and at night you had a slot bucket[1] by the bed. During the week, you had the basin where you just washed up. Then we moved to Anderson Street and stayed there until Cloverdale was established. But regardless where we lived, all of our neighborhoods were family.

Everybody knew each other. There was an elderly lady on the block who got sick and my sister took food to her everyday. She nursed her. She did everything. Everybody looked out for everybody. And everybody was your mother. We had to speak to everybody. We didn't have cars back then, and we walked. They used to call 'em stoops, they didn't call 'em a porch, they called 'em a stoop. And people sat on the stoop, and we had to speak. Good evening, good evening, good evening. And if you did something, anybody could spank you and yo mother would say, "Okay, if she spanked you then you did something. What did you do?" There wasn't jumping on the neighbor.

And we left our doors open, our windows open. We slept all night with the windows up. We could go into a neighbor's house and leave the house open, and nobody bothered it.

FLORRIE SCRIVEN

I had two children, a boy and a girl. I raised them in Yamacraw. It was very family-oriented, a close-knit community. Lot of love, lot of fun. All the neighbors knew each other. It had its little problems, but not like it is now.

CURT WILLIAMS

We was more uniformed [together] than the young people is today.

---

1. The formal name for a slot bucket is a chamber pot and was a portable toilet used at night prior to indoor plumbing.

WEST BROAD STREET

There's a running joke that if you want to know where any city's ghetto is, just find Martin Luther King Jr. Blvd. But that wasn't always the case in Savannah. MLK, then called West Broad Street, extending from Bay Street to Exchange Street, was once a corridor of thriving black neighborhoods and businesses. There was even a black-owned bank, originally called the Wage Earners' Bank. Opened in 1914, by 1920, it was one of the most prosperous banks owned and operated by persons of color in the country by 1920 with customers in almost every state. It was the first black bank in U.S. history to accumulate over $1M in assets. W.E.B. DuBois, in his *Crises* Magazine, said it helped more Negro business ventures to success than any other Negro bank.

West Broad Street was one of the most beautiful and powerful expressions of community in Savannah *black then*. Sticking together wasn't limited to opening your doors to family members or looking out for your neighbor's children. It was also supporting one another's entrepreneurial endeavors. Black people gave each other places of community, yes, but also safety and economic support.

If you had a friend who was a seamstress, then that's where you got your clothes from. If a brother in the neighborhood opened a bank, then that's where you saved your money. If a black mechanic opened a shop nearby, then that's who serviced your car. As Ms. Mary Butler Smith described the respective white and black worlds, "it was just two separate climates." That's not to say that black Savannahians didn't support the white climate. It's just that, if there was a black-owned option, then they took advantage of it. And there was one main street in Savannah that housed most black-owned brick and mortars, West Broad Street. It came up in every single interview, sometimes without my asking anything about it.

Cruising down the corridor today, which was renamed Martin Luther King in 1990, you'll find only five black-owned businesses from the boulevard's beginning to its end. That wasn't always the case.

CAROLYN DOWSE

West Broad Street was thriving. It was the hub. That was our area.

MARY BUTLER SMITH

The whole area was black. There was some whites there who wanted to make money and didn't mind being around black folks. Funeral homes, churches, everything in that area, and my daddy's tire shop was there too. Across the street, there was a white man who owned a confectionery store, and the building on the next corner was a fish market.

FLORRIE SCRIVEN

Matthew Fish Market. Prices was different then, of course. The fishermen would bring them and dump them on the stall and then we could select which fish we want. And then they even sold fish head. It was sold separate. They also had the chicken farm store with live chicken. We had two movie theaters, Star and Dunbar.

RUBY JONES

I went to the theaters all the time. A girl went to Beach High with me, she was in a movie with Harry Belafonte and somebody else. Her name was Marilyn. She was a pretty girl. West Broad Street used to jump. There was a lot of clubs, restaurants, stores.

CAROLYN DOWSE

Yackum and Yackum was like...that's where we bought all our clothes. This record sto', Sam's Record Store. We had all the black-owned businesses. You know Bynes Royall was over there. It wasn't [just] Bynes, because Frank came out the Army and then he went into business with Royall. See the Royall family still has investments, so that's where Bynes Royall come from. They were on West Broad at one time back then too, where Wendy's is now, it was up in there.

Bynes and Royall is the oldest black business in the city of Savannah, and it's the longest black-owned running funeral home in the state of Georgia. It's currently located at 204 West Hall Street.

FLORRIE SCRIVEN

We had Old Savannah Pharmacy. That was our drug store. Then we had Duke's [a drug store], which was on Congress Street.

CURT WILLIAMS

Every night club was run by blacks. Now the white folks owned the building. We had two tailor shops, which one of 'em is still in progress. It's National Tailors. It's run by Jews. 'Cross the street you had a shop that used to tailor our clothes. It was also run by Jews. Then we had only one black studio to take pictures. He wasn't a Jew. He was a Greek or something. And other than that, everything was black.

Where Wendy's is, that was the Union Train Station. They used to come in from Florida, put you out at the Union Station. A lil further down was the round house. You go there, turn the trains around, go back wherever. The overpass where SCAD don' built all them buildings, that was where you catch the train in the morning to go to Atlanta and you come back in the afternoon.

In 2015, GPB featured a story called "Savannah Residents Remember Frogtown and Old West Broad Street." In it, they referred to Union Station as the "pillar of the community and a beautiful work of architecture." Union Station was yet another source of pride and inspiration for the residents who lived around it and the citizens who patronized the area.

Where the I-16 exit ramp currently ends, that used to be Frogtown, where a community of freed slaves settled after the Civil War. Frogtown neighbors were a village, and as the West African proverb points out, that's what it takes to a raise a child. In the GPB interview, former Frogtown resident, Jestine Winford, drove home how much of a family they were. "Everybody was yo mother, everybody. We didn't have a telephone, but Mama would know what I did on the hill before I got down on the bottom."

As the saying goes, though, there are always two sides to a story. As glamorous as West Broad Street was to many, Steven Williams saw it differently.

STEVEN WILLIAMS

> It was a dump. Nothing but greasy spoons and juke joints, but people put a little bit of class on it now. It was historical because that's where all the black businesses were, you know. If you was a black lawyer, that's where you were. If you was in real estate and black, that's where you were. That's where everybody was at. But it wasn't no high class place, no fancy place. But that's where it was at. Every town you went in, it was the same way. When I was travelling in the Air Force, all you had to do was get to the train station or the bus station, find a porter. "Hey man, where's the place?" And he'd know exactly what you were talking about. He could direct you to the place.

There was a reason why West Broad became a dump. In 1963, residents and entrepreneurs on West Broad Street were ordered to leave by the City of Savannah for the construction of I-16 and the housing projects, Kayton and Frazier Homes. Although the interstate arrived in the '60s and immediately uprooted many residents, the businesses didn't leave as quickly. They hung around, though barely, for another 25 or so years, until the '90s, when ironically the street turned into a boulevard named after the beloved civil rights leader, who often visited Savannah. Because it took some years between the flyover (also known as an overpass) being built and the businesses closing, I believe many felt the collapse was due to a lack of support, as did Florrie:

FLORRIE SCRIVEN

> Something like the white man's ice is colder. We started shopping elsewhere like on Broughton Street and all of these places, and eventually they just had to close in.

That wasn't necessarily the case. The Savannah Metropolitan Planning Committee stated that while the intent of the flyover and the housing projects was to simply improve transportation and add affordable housing, they didn't predict that it would end up disconnecting streets and hindering economic development.

CURT WILLIAMS

> A lot of them old buildings, old clubs, they still standing, but they all boarded up. A lot of our roots is right here. We owned a lot of stuff, but we was pushed out.

CAROLYN DOWSE

> It's just so sad the way it really deteriorated.

"Krak teet fa 'eel 'e bodi en soul en myne"
—Hermina Glass-Hill
(speak for the healing of the body and soul and mind)

CHAPTER SIX

BEATING THE SYSTEM TOGETHER

"Got to ease yo foot out the lion's mouth, a lil at a time." -Gloria "Puff" Washington

No matter what happened, our struggles and efforts could not eradicate the weight of two hundred years. Children and grandchildren of slaves could not converse or compete with children of planters, descendants of London barristers, or upward climbing white Americans. When trying to survive was your number one goal and barely getting by was your reality, it was difficult and impractical even to fill your home with books and discuss theories across the dinner table.

That's still the case today for too many persons of color in Savannah. More than half of the city's population of more than 147,000 is black, and more than 22,000 black Savannahians live in poverty. The reasoning is simple. Before 1865, most black people were enslaved, earning no money, property, or education. After slavery, many sharecropped, earning little to no money, property, or education. After sharecropping, those same black folks and their descendants transitioned to menial, low-paying jobs. Oftentimes, children didn't finish school because they had to drop out for work to help with home expenses. Black schools simply didn't have the resources to give a quality education.

Furthermore, before the Equal Opportunity Act of 1972, employers were outright refusing to hire people because they were black and/or female. On top of that, black people have been colliding with laws aimed at black and poor people, called Black Codes, since the end of slavery. You could be arrested, for instance, for spitting on the sidewalk, not having at least a dollar in your pocket, defending yourself from a white person's attack, challenging discrimination, or simply being at the wrong place at the wrong time.

All of this—combined with post-traumatic slave syndrome[1] —leads to chronic stress, mental illness, physical ailments, poverty, and more. For generations on top of generations, the descendants of enslaved people have been relegated to the bare minimum (and sometimes not even that). The descendants of slave owners, on the other hand, didn't (and don't) have half, a third, or even a fourth of these problems to deal with. When that's the case, when the people who make the laws and cut the checks look like you, then you're in a better position to succeed. If your ancestors weren't slaves but slave-owners, running businesses without having to pay laborers, then you're even in an even higher position to succeed.

Research historic Savannah houses, and you'll find pictures of two and three-story mansions made of stone or grey brick, ornamented with sprawling porches and grand entrances, intricate iron work, and columns that seem to demand a bow. These homes were in large part built by slave-owning millionaires then inherited by heirs who'd occupy the homes or turn them into museums, restaurants, and inns.

Though Savannah's wealth was built on the backs of Blacks, hardly any lived the extravagant lifestyle that tourists flock to Savannah to photograph. For many Black Savannahians in the 1930s, when the grandchildren of slaves were being born and raised under the grip of the Great

Depression, the reality was that "families lived on less than two hundred dollars a year in leaky, tin-roofed houses lacking either glass or screens in the windows. It was a world in which children walked miles to rickety schools and the elderly walked miles to rickety churches. It was a world in which farmers borrowed small sums at indefinite rates of interest and lost their lands at indefinite rates of foreclosure" (Drums and Shadows, 1986).

Mr. Steven Williams's family was a prime example of that poverty. He reminded me very much of my father—small in stature with a huge personality and sense of humor, high yellow as he'd be described in New Orleans, with glossy eyes that you can't quite call grey or blue but maybe something in between. In my five or so times meeting with him, I'd never seen him without his oxygen machine or a smile. Of all my elders, Mr. Williams was most interested in the book release and often requested updated versions of the manuscript. He grew up in Tatemville, a neighborhood in West Savannah.

STEVEN WILLIAMS

> I was born in this house 81 years ago. Tatemville was a rough place then. It wasn't rough because of gangs or anything. It was just rough living. I think city limits came as far as 60th Street, and it was actual farms out here. That was a watermelon patch all through there [pointing out the window]. They used to call this section of Savannah 'the dirt farmers.' That means we was the lowest of the lowest. They even called us that in high school, at Haven Home. You always got the worst end because you was a dirt farmer. That was all we was fit for, in they mind.

MADIE UNDERWOOD

> We lived in the house on Norton Street twice. Things was so hard and so tight financially, and daddy wasn't able to pay his rent sometimes. And back then, the white man would put a sign on your house for rent. Right across your front door, and he'd give you a certain amount of time to find another place, or he'd just come and move you out. So Daddy had to move, and he moved on Scarborough Street, and so things so bad there that a fella came and put a For Rent on that house and he moved back in the first house.

Ms. Carolyn Dowse is one of the last elders I interviewed. Though over 80 years old, she is always full of energy and on the go. She is neither shy nor shameful about any subject, and her voice is loud enough to make sure she got her point across the first time. A school teacher turned principal and administrator turned ordained minister and marriage counselor turned nonprofit consultant—her abundant present in no way mirrors her humble past.

CAROLYN DOWSE, 85 YEARS OLD

> I came along where I used to have holes in my shoes because we walked every place. I was considered to be poor, and I think this is another thing that sort of made me feel as if I wasn't as good as other people. My sister Sadie Cartledge sat me down and she said, "You are as good as the president of the United States. Do not get in your mind that you're not."

They went without, not because they didn't work hard or refused to "pull themselves up by their bootstraps," but because they weren't being paid as they should have been. Sadie Cartledge, who raised Carolyn, was also a school teacher turned principal. Yet, the child she was raising wore shoes with holes at the bottom.

Togetherness was instrumental in surviving racism and mid-20th century discrimination, poverty, poor health, police brutality, and internalized biases like colorism. To demonstrate the complexities and layers of racism and discrimination, it's important to understand that neither racism nor discrimination began in the Jim Crow era, when laws ensured that the men and women who were once enslaved would never level out with that of their former owners. Racism was created to justify slavery, to override morals with "science" and social norms. If a child grew up seeing black people being relegated to second-class citizenship, then that child—white or black—will accept it as reality.

MADIE UNDERWOOD

> When I was young, coming up, as an adolescent teenager, maybe before adolescent age, but when I was coming up, there was just black schools and white schools and black teachers and white teachers, black neighborhoods and white neighborhoods and etcetera etcetera. Everything was divided and the black people was like a minority under the white people. The white people acted like they were supreme over

the black race. That's the way they treated us when I was coming up, so that's all I knew.

CAROLYN DOWSE

On the corner of St. John's Baptist Church, that big, brick building? St. John's Villa? That's where I went to school. Although I lived in the 700-block of Anderson Street and Anderson Street School [now SCAD's Anderson Hall] was in the 500-block, it was an all-white school, so I had to walk way to East Broad, which is where St. John's Villa is today.

STEVEN WILLIAMS

It was real serious when I was coming along. Real serious. If you was a black girl, you had a lot of problems. I wish somebody could write a book about the black woman, especially during segregation. She was really something. Those women had to walk to work, go clean up people's houses for maybe five or six dollars a week, and had to come home and cook for us and do the same thing everyday. It was a struggle for a black woman. Black women really caught hell.

The hell that black women caught didn't just spring up once they started jobs and families. It followed them from a girlhood that was often snatched too soon. Black girls were and still are treated like women. According to a Georgetown Law study, "Adults view Black girls as less innocent and more adult-like than their white peers, especially in the age range of 5–14." As a result, black girls face harsher penalties in discipline and greater use of force. While the disciplinary part of the study was referring to the school and justice system, this traumatizing perception and disparagement of black girls has also led to disproportionate physical and sexual violence at home, at school, on the job, and in the neighborhood.

STEVEN WILLIAMS

A woman, or a girl, they really caused her hell on the streets. Especially if they was married, going to work, somebody hitting on 'em. 'Cause they had to walk so far, you know? Guys hitting on 'em. Not only just black guys, but white guys. And when they get to the job, the owner of the house hitting on 'em. And then she's got all of this stuff back here. Four kids. But she's got to walk to work everyday. My mama did house work and it was easy to remember that because that's all they did. Teaching too, but they didn't make no money.

SADIE GREEN

The white man would give you a job if you go to bed with him. Then you can work for 'em. But if you couldn't go to bed with him, then you ain't had no job. That's like slavery time. White folks ain't just going to black women. They been doing that all they life. Myself, my four cousins and my cousin's brother, we traveled together, so they couldn't harm us three girls. We was lucky. So many during that time, 13 years old on to 18 up black girls having white babies.

The Georgetown Law study said the exact same thing about black boys. They are viewed as adults far too soon. Black girls and boys are forced to mentally mature faster than their white peers. Being trained how to survive in the world because of your skin color is just something that white children cannot relate to, and Mr. Williams' story supports that.

STEVEN WILLIAMS

If you was a black boy you had major problems. I remember my mother used to tell us—we had small sidewalks then, real narrow sidewalks—if you was walking, always yield for the white person. But if it's a white woman, you don't want to get nowhere close to her. You accidentally butt into her, touch her, or something like that, you was in trouble. My mother used to tell us if a white woman is approaching, you go to the other side of the street. Cross over. Don't that sound crazy? I'd say, 'Mama, what if I meet another one on the other side?' Cross again. You keep crossing. And you walked in the street at night back then, you walk in the middle of the street. Not the shadows with a hoodie on. You walked in the middle of the street. For a black boy, it was real dangerous. And those old folks used to tell us about it. 'Don't you go down that street.'

You was nothing.

MADIE UNDERWOOD

When we did get a chance to go out and enjoy ourselves at all, if you went to a restaurant, you had to go in through the back. They had White Only on the restaurants. And some of them would serve colored people too and they'd say colored with an arrow pointing to the back. And sometimes you could go in the back and get your food and sometimes they'd give it to you out a window.

If you went to a movie, you couldn't go to a white movie at all. What they used to call a show. When you went there, you had your own movie and they had theirs. When we ride the bus, we had the one long seat. The back seat is a long seat, in the back of the bus. They had that seat and one seat above it on both sides, was where the black people had to sit. If the whole bus was empty, we could not sit. We had to just stand because those were the white people seats. We weren't allowed to sit in them at all.

That's the way the bus situation was. And that wasn't just the city buses. That was the highway buses too, once they hit the south at a certain point. Certain seats, you couldn't sit on. Now, while we're traveling, after we moved up north, traveling back down south, when you get to a certain point, that was the same system on the highway and everywhere else. White only bathrooms and they had colored bathrooms. They had arrows pointing where you was supposed to go.

And a lot of times they wasn't hardly fit to go in. Most times they was unsanitary. So with my pride, when we go home to visit our parents, my husband's parents was in Savannah too, we didn't take our kids to those bathrooms. We would stop off the highway somewhere and let our kids eliminate themselves that way. We wouldn't even take them in those places until they lifted that.

Racism wasn't hidden. Its face, words, and actions didn't leave you second-guessing. Your public bathroom was dirtier because you were black, your water fountain rustier, your schoolbook more outdated, your seat in the back of the bus, and your stores less equipped.

Every ism—racism included—has its extreme. The Ku Klux Klan was (and still is) the racist extremists. Founded in 1866, the Ku Klux Klan (KKK) existed in almost every southern state by 1870. After slavery ended, a lot of whites feared that the formerly enslaved would rise up and retaliate physically and politically, now that they'd been granted the right to vote and run for office due to Reconstruction efforts.

Slaves turned sharecroppers were also beginning to unionize, demanding better wages and work environments.

As a means of maintaining white supremacy and subjugating blacks, the KKK—with their white sheets with pointed hoods to conceal their identity—rose up to make sure none of that happened. And they did so through violence and intimidation. By legal definition, a street gang consists of three or more people who meet regularly, exercise crimes, show their unity by way of symbols or dress, and are territorial. The KKK is a gang of terrorists who uphold their beliefs through bloodshed and the threat of it.

Black schools, churches, and homes—anywhere that symbolized or demonstrated black independence—were targeted by the KKK. By the end of 1876, they had won the political majority across the South. Then D.W. Griffith released the film *Birth of a Nation*, depicting black men as angry drunks who killed white men and raped white women. Who saved the day? The Klan.

More powerful than politics is art, and this film and *The Clansman*, the book that the film was adapted from, revived the Ku Klux Klan. Unlike their predecessors, the revived generation of white terrorists had more guns, bombs even, and a stronger media and civic presence to make sure everyone knew what they were capable of.

MATILDA "PATT" BROWN, 80 YEARS OLD

> The Klu Klux Klan have come down 34th Street. We lived at 641 West 34th Street, and they come on down to West Broad. They were in the white sheets, walking at night, tryna scare folk. I can remember them having a cross and walking with it. It was something else, you know?

All the elders interviewed for this book were at least 18 years old in 1955. I used that year, an extremely tumultuous one, as a marker to zoom in on the environment in which they were growing into adulthood. In Savannah, that meant constant police brutality. Although Savannah hired its first black officers in 1947 to combat this issue, there were only nine of them and they were constrained to certain areas of the city. Black officers couldn't arrest white citizens, but white officers could pretty much do as they pleased with black citizens sans punishment. So in a 1955 submission of complaints (and proposed solutions) to Mayor Mingledorff, one of the chief requests was for hiring more black police officers.

In 1947, the city's first set of black police officers was hired. There were 60 candidates to begin with, who were all judged on their character, intelligence, and military service. That 60 slashed down to 16 when it was time for training, which took place at the old Masonic Temple and was conducted by white judges and lawyers. Whether or not seven of those 16 were dismissed or voluntarily stepped down, I don't know, but only nine ended up being sworn in. They came to be called The Original Nine. The Original Nine, it turns out, were the first black police officers to be hired in the entire state of Georgia.

Their powers were very constrained though. For one, they could only patrol black neighborhoods. They surely couldn't arrest white people. Like their other skinfolk, they were still subjected to Jim Crow laws. James Rodgers, the police chief who'd recruited them, requested that The Original Nine be his pallbearers. (A year after they were hired, Rodgers learned that his health was failing.) Lieutenant John White of The Original Nine recalled in an interview with GPB that "they were only allowed to carry the casket to the church doors but not inside because of segregation" (Chen, 2016).

The Original Nine weren't hired because the whites in power thought it was time. They were hired after being pressured by the black community. One of the main reasons for requesting black officers—in addition to equal opportunity—was to curb police brutality. White men had proven themselves time and again that they couldn't be trusted to protect and serve those with darker complexions. Oftentimes, they only brought more pain and violence into the neighborhoods. So black folk reasoned that if their own kind were in positions of power, then the injustices wouldn't occur. While I'm sure having black officers patrol black neighborhoods cut down on mistreatment, it did not eliminate it altogether. Curt Williams told me about some of the underhandedness that used to go on:

CURT WILLIAMS

> And they knew blacks, on Fridays and Saturdays nights, was gon' fill the clubs. Come out the driveway, the police sitting right there.
> "Boy, have you been drinking?" "Yes, suh."
> "How much you had, son?" *Sniff, sniff.* "I'ma have to write you a ticket. I'll tell you what. Just gimme $20 and we'll overlook the ticket."

Serving more than four decades some of them, they did a lot of good in the community, which is why black folks in 1955 requested even more black officers to be hired. Requests to Mayor Mingledorff also included hiring black women to handle black women inmates, appointing a black person to the Board of Education to represent the needs of the black community, building more housing for low-income families, and paving more streets and installing storm drainages in black neighborhoods (Hoskins, 2013).

The national climate for black people in America was also rough. In 1955, Emmett Till, a 14-year-old black boy from

Chicago, was sent to Mississippi for the summer by his mother. Three days after his arrival, Carolyn Bryant, a white woman, accused Till of confronting her in an aggressively sexual way. Her husband and another accomplice tortured then shot Emmett to death, and were acquitted of all charges. In 2017, at the age of 82, Bryant admitted in an interview that she'd lied. A month after Emmett's murderers were acquitted, Rosa Parks, a trained demonstrator and NAACP secretary, was arrested for not giving up her bus seat to a white man. Her arrest catapulted a successful bus boycott of the Montgomery bus system, of which 70 percent of its patrons were black.

MADIE UNDERWOOD

> Like Rosa Parks and the other people that was in the limelight, when they was coming along and they was in the right place at the right time doing the same thing, that was happening all over the south. I was involved, personally, in some of that myself. As far as rebelling, just tired of people treating you bad.

STEVEN WILLIAMS

> We would have to ask for a job, "Do you got anything for us to do?" You had certain statements you had to make. You never asked a white man what you'd make because you wouldn't get the job. You work a while then you find some more black people around and ask them what you were getting paid. That's the way it was. You just took whatever work you could get. I have worked on places even where they call you nigger all day long. And you smile.

ROOSEVELT ROUSE

> I stayed at Derst Bakery for 23 years. I guess you can say I had trouble. I know it was 'bout the bathroom 'cause see back then you go in one side and the white man go in another side. See what I'm saying? I was in a hurry, so I went in they side. And a white man come up and start raising hell with me. I said, man, I ain't got to take this shit, and I ain't gon' take it. And I left. I didn't let nobody push me around. That's all there is to it. I didn't get fired now. I just left.

A powerful difference between the days of Roosevelt and those of his parents and grandparents, for instance, was the ability to just walk out when feeling disrespected. The disrespect ran deep though, not just socially but institutionally. Whites limited black Savannah's access to employment, political offices, and other rights and privileges such as being treated equal to whites in public facilities which their tax dollars supported and in local businesses where they spent their money.

A common response to that problem is asking why black people didn't (or don't) just build their own facilities. They did. They were taken from them, time after time, whether burned down, destroyed, or uprooted by eminent domain. The issue isn't black folk refusing to build, or not being self-reliant, but that the powers that be did not allow us to keep our own. Instead, we were consistently put in inferior positions and forced to rely on the same powers that be.

In 1929, for instance, a man named Louis Ellis was evicted from his home for not paying his rent on time. Instead of jumping back in the cycle of working jobs that didn't pay enough to cover his basic expenses, he petitioned the city for a piece of vacant land off of Wheaton and Liberty. They approved it, so he built a small house made of scraps and had gardens around it. Soon after, others followed.

RUBY JONES

> Liberty and East Broad Street, that's where Tin City was. The black people was po, and they build—I don't know where all the tin came from—shelter and things for themselves. They had gardens and everything, and I don't know who came by and saw that, but they changed it into the projects so the people could have a decent place to live.

Tin City was a village of tiny houses, community gardens, organic fruit and vegetables, composting. It even had a mayor. I'm sure it wasn't physically comfortable, especially in extreme weather, but its residents proved what's possible when everybody worked together, because it worked for more than 30 years.

In 1962, the city reclaimed the land and built the Herbert Kayton Homes Projects.

---

1. Post-traumatic stress disorder is a result of being shocked, scared, or put in an extremely dangerous situation, be it mental, emotional, and/or physical. It's often diagnosed in those who've been to war, have survived school and workplace shootings, or have been victims of abuse at home. Post-traumatic slave syndrome is the result of generational oppression stemming from slavery. Centuries of abuse, degradation, family separation, institutionalized racism, and the unpunished killings of black bodies without any mental/emotional therapy or reparations led to what is now known as post-traumatic slave syndrome, a term coined by Dr. Joy DeGruy.

CHAPTER SEVEN

BLACK SAVANNAH VS. BROUGHTON STREET

"But black people, oh man. Black people had so much pride." -Steven Williams

Dick Gregory used a powerful analogy to describe what was happening in black communities across the country: *The Negro has a callus growing on his soul and it's getting harder and harder to hurt him there...Like a callus on a foot in a shoe that's too tight. The foot is nature's, and that shoe was put on by man. That tight shoe will pinch your foot and make you holler and scream. But sooner or later, if you don't take the shoe off, a callus will form on the foot and begin to wear out the shoe. It's the same with the Negro in America today... Unless that system is adjusted to fit him, too, that callus is going to wear out that system.*

By the early 1960s, West Broad Street began closing in, falling into blight. Where lively established homes and businesses once stood, they were now rundown and abandoned. First came the ghetto label then the announcement of urban renewal followed by new constructions.

This sequence didn't just happen in Savannah though. Historically black neighborhoods and business districts all over the country were being gutted in the same manner.

Black Wall Street in Durham, North Carolina mirrored that of West Broad Street. Durham's Black Wall Street also collapsed in the early 1960s in the name of "urban renewal," which included the construction of Highway 147.

The Black Wall Street in Tulsa, Oklahoma lived the same outcome. Following the Tulsa riots, Tulsa's Black Wall Street bounced back stronger than ever, but an interstate overpass was built, cutting straight through Greenwood Avenue, the hub's primary street.

The Hill District, an African-American community in Pittsburgh, suffered the same fate in 1956 when over 8,000 families and 400 businesses were removed for a new civic arena. The Cypress Freeway in Oakland, California, opening in 1957, birthed the same consequence for black residents and business owners there. The same would go for Central East Austin, Texas and Bayview Hunter's Point in San Francisco and the Tremé neighborhood of New Orleans. The list goes on and on.

After West Broad Street closed in, everyone began shopping on Broughton Street, a thriving corridor of shops and restaurants owned by whites. While blacks were pretty much always allowed to shop on Broughton Street, neither working there nor eating were allowed. You could order food, but it had to be go.

LULA MAE POLITE

> I remember when Broughton Street had the white fountains and the negro ones. It used to be a Woolworth's. They used to sell food. And Kress. Kress used to sell food. They used to sell like candies and cookies and stuff like that. You could go in there and buy cookies and stuff, but sit down and eat? No, you couldn't do that.

DOROTHY PARRISH

When I came to Savannah, Broughton Street was nothing like it is today. When I came there, Cress was on one side of Broughton Street and McCrory was on the other, and JCPenneys was on one corner. The most thing that I can think about that was really enlightening to me was that the ladies then, most was white females, wore hats and gloves downtown to shop. And as you know, we was not allowed to go in the stores to have a soda or to have a hamburger.

Segregation and discrimination were all over the nation. In response, black folk began organizing and mobilizing, coming together to decide as a team what they wanted and how to get it. In this case, it was equal access and treatment. Many became active members of regional and national efforts toward freedom and autonomy for African Americans including the National Association for the Advancement of Colored People (NAACP) and the Southern Christian Leadership Conference (SCLC).

Westley Wallace Law, better known as W.W. Law, born and raised in Savannah (and a proud Gullah Geechee man) served as the president of Savannah's NAACP chapter from 1950 to 1976. He got involved in the organization, as many young folk did, when he was in high school. He credited much of his inspiration for advocating for his community to hearing the stories of elders born into slavery or who fought in the Civil War. Inspiration also came from growing up poor, despite how hard he and his mother worked, and being treated as inferior during his Army service.

After his military service ended and he graduated from Georgia State Industrial College (now Savannah State University), he applied to teach in the local school system. He was denied because of his affiliation with the NAACP. So he took a federal job with the post office, becoming a mailman.

MS. PUSCHA-SCOTT

> Mr. Law kept us involved. He was a friend of the family. He was my brother's boy scout leader and a wonderful postman, I tell you. Mr. Law was connected with everything, a wonderful person. He just had his hands on everything. He was for the youth and for the adults, everyone. He was just for our history. He was a walking encyclopedia, full of information. Very humble.

W.W. Law became successful in organizing black Savannah. When the community had a complaint or a demand against the city, the mayors met with Law, the spokesperson of the people. One of his most successful efforts was the Broughton Street boycott, after two Beach High students and one Savannah State student—Carolyn Quinn, Joan Tyson, and Ernest Robinson—were arrested for trying to eat at a whites-only lunch counter at Levy's Department Store on Broughton Street.

More sit-ins were scheduled, but police closed the stores before the students arrived. Again, you could shop there and order your food to go, but you couldn't eat or work there. Black folk had enough and called a larger boycott. No shopping on Broughton Street, period, until they started letting us shop, work, and eat there (and stopped calling adults boy or girl).

The NAACP, under W. W. Law's leadership, arranged for older, property-owning blacks to bail out the younger foot soldiers when they were arrested. As Florrie Scriven said, who also did a number of sit-ins, said: "We stuck together."

Two days into the boycott, *Savannah Morning News* reported: "These lunch counter demonstrations are both unwise and unfortunate...We do not think any member of the community, white or black, wishes to inspire violence, yet these sit downs pose this threat." But the sit-ins (then called sit-downs) continued.

CAROLYN DOWSE

> Do not go on Broughton Street for Christmas to buy any Christmas gifts. [Law] said, if you have any credit cards or anything, pay them off and don't charge anything. The blacks worked with him one hundred percent. We needed pantyhose and all, we were sending up north to our families, and nobody shopped on Broughton Street.

In June 1960, *The Chicago Defender* reported that the boycott had cost merchants more than $1,000,000. The next month, two hundred and fifty robed klansmen paraded Broughton Street and threw bricks into NAACP members' houses with notes that said: "Keep away from our goddamn stores black niggers. White folks can live without you goddamn black niggers money." *Savannah Tribune* responded, "The colored community refuses to be intimidated by men who parade under the disguise of hoods on Broughton Street."

In addition to W.W. Law, leaders like Benjamin Van Clarke and Hosea Williams were equally essential to the struggle. Hosea Williams had a pretty rough life coming up. At 14, he was accused of being involved with a white girl and had to run away to avoid being lynched. When he came of age, he enlisted in the Army and served in World War II, where he was injured to the extent that it left him with a permanent limp. After his four-year term, he earned his high school diploma and then a Bachelor's in Chemistry from Morris Brown College and a

Master's in Chemistry from Atlanta University (now Clark-Atlanta University).

Lula Mae described Williams as a firm, outspoken man. "He just wasn't scared to speak." He was nearly beaten to death for drinking from a white's only water fountain and spent over a month in the hospital recovering. Later, he lost his job at the Department of Agriculture for *krackin' his teet* against racism. Witnessing his children being refused service at Savannah lunch counters on account of their skin, he decided to join the local NAACP chapter, where he served as Vice President under W.W. Law.

Law disagreed with the night marches and militant approach that Williams favored. So Williams resigned from the NAACP, stating that with or without its support, negroes were "ready to do something within the bounds of the U.S. Constitution to bring about full equality and full citizenship." With the encouragement of Martin Luther King, Jr., he established Savannah's chapter of the Southern Christian Leadership Conference.

Under the SCLC, Williams led an organization called the Chatham County Crusade for Voters to register black people to vote. Several whites acquired peace warrants[1] against him, saying that the night marches he led kept them up at night. A white woman said that the protests made her fear for her life. Each formal complaint was tallied, and Williams was thrown in jail for 65 days. Over the course of his life, he was arrested more than 125 times. After his arrest, riots broke out.

For the same reason that folk set fire to Harlem in 1964, Los Angeles in 1965, Detroit in 1967, D.C. in '68, and Augusta in 1970, Savannah felt the heat too. Black people were mad as hell. Housing was terrible, education was bad, police brutality was ridiculous, and unemployment was sky high. All it took was a final straw. That straw for black Savannah was Hosea Williams being arrested on what everyone knew were bogus charges and held longer than any other civil rights leaders ever.

His bond amounted to $30,000, the equivalent of about $247,000 in 2018. His followers boycotted, protested, then burned Sears and Firestone stores down. The flames got them the response they were looking for. "After the Sears, Roebuck and Firestone stores were burned, Citizens and Southern Bank President Mills B. Lane, Jr., stepped in as a mediator and made it possible for Williams to get out of jail" (Grant, 2001). Mills B. Lane, Jr., along with several other white businessmen, came together to form the Committee of 100 to not only have Williams released but to finally integrate the rest of the city. Upon release, Williams told Lane that if the protesters' demands for integration and just treatment were not met, then he would be right back in jail the next day.

FLORRIE SCRIVEN

Every day, twice a day, we were involved in the civil rights movement. In fact my sister and I, we were the first ones to integrate Broughton Street. Nobody knew about that. We worked with Hosea Williams. We had our little office [for organizing the movement] up over The Blue Room, a black club on West Broad Street. It's destroyed now. It's no longer there. And the office was up over that club.

I marched twice a day. They put me on the front because I had a loud voice and I could sing, so I was on the front line, twice a day. Even when Bobby Hill was arrested, we were marching and having meetings at the YMCA, and then we would march near the old jail on Habersham Street. That's where they used to house the prisoners, and they had Bobby Hill in there. That was our civil rights lawyer."

I was so blessed that, where I was working, my supervisor, a white woman, would let me leave. I was working at Memorial Medical Center as a nurse. Her son now has the floral shop, John Davis.

With [Benjamin Van] Clark and all of us, we used to go around and the first day that they declared segregation, my sister and I, Lula and I, Big Al, one other gentlemen, and my daughter's grandmother, Hosea told us to dress up so we could go and sit in. So we went to what was one of the elite's restaurants, Anton's. It was next to the Savannah Bank at the time on Abercorn and Broughton. We went and sat in there, and was treated very, very highly among all the other ones. We went back to report that night how things went with us, and that night he said, "Y'all go to another club." So we went to Johnnie Ganems. I think it's on Abercorn. It's still there. My sister and I, all of us, went back.

Eighteen months later, Mayor Mingledorff resigned due to the pressure, and the *Savannah Morning News* reported that five stores chose bankruptcy over integration.

The young protesters were specific in their demands: desegregation of all lunch counters, water fountains, restrooms, and dressing rooms. They wanted to be addressed by whites with courtesy titles such as missus and mister (instead of gal and boy). They wanted employment of black salespersons and an end to persecution of demonstrators.

Not all acts of resistance were organized. This is a critical part of black history too often left out of textbooks and Black History Month. Not all activists were involved in the NAACP or the SCLC. Some didn't even consider themselves "activists" or otherwise involved in the civil rights movement. They were just...sick and tired.

MADIE UNDERWOOD

When I was 14 [in 1946], and I had to leave school and go to work, I was working at Desoto Hilton, which still exists. After I left work, I had to go home and do chores before I do my school work. Now I'm very tired. I'm tired. I got on the bus, the bus packed full of people. People was actually standing up. And so there was one seat behind the bus driver and I sat in it, and I wasn't allowed to do that.

When I did it, the whole bus was in a uproar. The driver was yelling at me, the white people yelling at me, the black people yelling. Everybody yelling. One black man all the way in the back say, "These young people just starting a lot of trouble. They just causing all of these problems, and we don't need these problems. Just come back here. You can have my seat." And I was rebellious at that time. I told him, "I don't need your seat. I have one. You didn't offer it to me when I got on the bus." I figured I paid my fare just like everybody else, so I got a seat. The driver said, "Well, I'm not moving until you get in your own place, where you supposed to be." I said, "Well, I'm tired. I don' been to school. I don' been to work. I wanna go home. I'm tired. I have a seat and you didn't charge me no less than you charged anybody else who got on this bus. I had to pay the same thing. I'm not getting up."

So he called the police. Back then, there were no black polices in Savannah, only white. There was no black bus drivers either, only white. And so the police came and he happened to be a person that sort of like agreed with me but couldn't really say it. He say, "Well, you're going to be behind schedule if you don't just keep moving. Maybe you should just keep moving." And he was talking to the bus driver. And when he got back off, they decided to move on.

Now during that time, we lived in West Savannah. And at a certain point in West Savannah, it was a white people's neighborhood. You don' passed the black people neighborhood and you going into the white people neighborhood. You go in the white people neighborhood rebelling, then you in big trouble. I had sense enough not to do that. So I passed my stop I was supposed to get off. And I rode the bus all the way to the end of the black people neighborhood then I got off and had to walk all the way back home.

Times were bad, but they gradually got better. Minds didn't change on their own though, and it wasn't a simple change of heart that sped up the desegregation process. It was people like Madie refusing to give up her seat. Florrie and her sister, Lula Mae marching twice a day. Hosea Williams and Benjamin Van Clarke being beaten with police batons and thrown in jail, and still refusing to let up on their demands for their people. W.W. Law writing to the federal government, asking them to stop funding Memorial Hospital until they desegregated their facilities. Broughton Street stores buckling one after the other due to boycotts. Protestors inciting the formation of the Committee of 100. It was as civil rights leader, Fannie Lou Hamer said best, black folk being "sick and tired of being sick and tired." Where injustice rested, hell was raised. And it worked.

In Fall of 1961, white business owners opened their lunch counters to blacks. This happened eight months before the Civil Rights Act was passed, which mandated white businesses to integrate. Afterwards, W. W. Law held a mass meeting one Sunday at St. Phillips AME to call off the 70-week boycott. Curtis V. Cooper, leader of the boycott committee, seconded the motion and no one dissented.

Black Savannah had won.

The demonstrations assigned by W. W. Law were nonviolent. But often demonstrators were not met with nonviolence, but were abused by citizens and by police. As Malcolm X put it, "We are nonviolent with people who are nonviolent with us." Otherwise, (also using X's words) "[i]t is criminal to teach a man not to defend himself when he is the constant victim of brutal attacks."

It's important to understand, though, that black people did not wait for Malcolm X to begin taking a more militant approach in defending their bodies and their liberties as human beings. Our rights did not come from begging and turning our cheeks when spat on and kicked. We fought every single day with our fists, our guns, our mouths, our wallets, our votes, and our prayers.

Although desegregation was a solid win for the people, there were still more wins to be had. Also during the boycott, and before the Civil Rights Act of 1964 was passed, a few other happenings occurred around the city:

- Thirty two sit-downers were arrested.
- Five more were arrested for refusing to vacate Levy's when asked to.
- The Ku Klux Klan burned two 18-foot crosses in Port Wentworth.
- City Council passed a new anti-picketing law.
- A carload of white men burned a cross at Hosea Williams's Thunderbolt home.
- The Crusade for Voters opened three schools for illiterate blacks.
- The NAACP's membership tripled.
- Mayor Malcolm McLean (after Mayor Mingledorff resigned) ended segregation in public libraries.
- Johnson High's principal, Alflorence Cheatham, was dismissed for participating in the Crusade of Votes. Sixty students protested his dismissal, and 23 were arrested.
- Six blacks were convicted of violating the state's unlawful assembly act by playing basketball at Daffin Park (the case had gone through three courts by this time).

- Mayor Maclean promised to employ more black policemen and place blacks on city commissions.
- Benjamin F. Lewis (Carolyn Dowse's brother) became the first black supervisor in the postal service.
- Eight more sit-downers were arrested.
- The U.S. Supreme Court overturned the conviction in the Daffin Park case.
- Seventeen white parents filed suit to prevent school integration then later launched a drive to open Savannah Country Day School.
- Judge Frank M. Scarlett ruled in the white parents' favor, stating that desegregation would cause more harm.

Another Savannah civil rights hero who's too often left out of conversations is John Saxon Pierce, also known as Piccolo, and more lovingly known as Bonk. He was right there with Hosea Williams, Benjamin Van Clark, W.W. Law, and even national leaders like Martin Luther King Jr., whose "I Have a Dream Speech" Piccolo made his way to D.C. to hear. Like his justice-demanding peers, he served time for his role in the struggle for equality. He was arrested for months, according to a *Savannah Morning News* article, for trying to integrate not schools, restaurants, or beaches, but *churches*. Like Savannah native Amelia Boynton Robinson, Piccolo was also present for the Bloody Sunday March of 1965 in Selma, Alabama.

You know that saying, "Everybody wants to be a chief"? That wasn't the case for Piccolo, content with doing whatever he could whenever he could. In his later years, that meant passing out flyers informing the people about what was going on and what they could do about it. "'Without people like Mr. Pierce,' [Mayor Otis Johnson] explained later, 'those numbers needed to drive the movement wouldn't have been reached. He was one of the people who organized locally' (Few, 2011).

Most people, though, knew Piccolo as the man always outside of the courthouse. Anyone else who attempted to spend hours on hours standing around outside of the courthouse would probably be asked to leave by the guarding police, but Piccolo was an exception.

FLORRIE SCRIVEN

Piccolo, that was one of the Civil Rights guy. He'd sit there in front of the courthouse all the time. He was the only one they allowed to sit there. He wasn't crazy at all. He was very respected. All the judges, lawyers, and everybody knew Piccolo. "Bonk, Bonk." When we go by, he'd call us Bonk Bonk. "Lemme have a dollar, Bonk Bonk, to get a sandwich." You can't refuse him. He was just that kind. Very wonderful personality and everything. They never had anything for him. Not like a park like they did for Clark, Benjamin Clark, or a center like W.W. Law or Mr. Delaware.

He passed away in 2011 at the age of 80. He doesn't have a park or recreation center named in his honor, as do his peers, but he does have a day commissioned by Chatham County. July 30th is Picollo Day.

---

1. A peace warrant is an arrest warrant that is issued after the complainant expresses just cause to fear that another person will commit an offense against their body or their property.

CHAPTER EIGHT

BLACK SAVANNAH VS. THE BOARD OF EDUCATION

"It shows you what you can do when you ain't supposed to be able to do it." -Steven Williams

For black people in America and the Caribbean, education is like religion. It isn't just about making a lot of money. Historically, education has been cherished as a key, a direct path to freedom. During slavery, it was illegal for us to be literate. Slaveowners feared that slaves would realize their position in life and rebel or escape by way of forged freedom papers and such. In *Slavery and Freedom in Savannah*, co-editors Leslie Harris and Daina Berry expound on the educating of blacks in antebellum Savannah. "Despite laws passed in 1817 by the city and in 1829 by the state that prohibited teaching free or enslaved blacks to read, secret schools for the education of blacks, free and enslaved, flourished in the antebellum period, led by free blacks who taught in their homes" (98). The book names Catherine Deveaux, Catherine's daughter Jane Deveaux, Julien Fromatin, James Porter, Mary Woodhouse, Mathilda Beasley, and James Simms as well-known underground black teachers during slavery. Simms, "a black teacher and later the historian of the First African Baptist Church, was whipped and fined for operating a school...."

After slavery ended in 1865, gaining an education still proved difficult for black people in Savannah. Abolitionists and philanthropists Harriet Ann Jacobs and William and Ellen Craft—former slaves who managed to escape—moved to Savannah after the Civil War to help the newly freed black folk transition more successfully into freedom. "They supplied food, clothing, medicine, and other essentials to hospital patients and refugees; they opened schools and orphanages; and they established homes for the elderly" (170). In 1870, the three established the Southern Industrial School and Labor Enterprise, which was burned down by the Ku Klux Klan the same year. Three years later, Jacobs and Crafts opened the Woodville Co-operative Farm School about thirty miles outside of Savannah in Bryan County, Georgia. "In 1876, resentful whites coordinated a smear campaign against the Crafts, accusing William of squandering donated school funds on his family's personal expenses" (170). He tried suing for libel but lost, and his reputation unfortunately couldn't be restored, resulting in his losing funding and eventually the school closing.

After more than ten generations of African Americans being denied an education, fifty years of legally being denied the right to read and write, and an ongoing struggle to organize and educate ourselves, in 1908 the state of Georgia imposed a literacy test and a poll tax as a means of depressing black men's right to vote and better their quality of life.[1] If it wasn't one thing, it was another. Resentful whites were determined to keep black people in the lowest rungs of society depending on white people for their survival, as in the days of slavery. These were the realities that my interviewees, their parents, and their parents dealt with.

When Ms. Madie shared how her parents were relegated to working jobs that didn't pay enough to consistently cover the daily expenses, I understood even more why my parents and grandparents stressed my getting an education. I understood why they hesitated when I explained that I was taking my son out of school to homeschool him. Ms. Madie's story reminded me of my mother wishing that her mother, who wasn't educated past elementary school, could've seen her graduate from college. I recalled her saying how proud my grandmother would have been to see me walk across two university stages. Education, for black folk, ain't a shrugging matter. Historically, it determined where on the ladder our livelihoods rested.

MADIE UNDERWOOD

> We was very poor. I didn't have much of anything, because Daddy was uneducated. So naturally, he had a low paying job. And Mama stayed home and took care of the kids, but she'd sew to make a lil money on the side. She would do other things for people, too, and they might hand her a dollar or two, here and there.

MS. PUSCHA-SCOTT

> Our parents gave us two choices: either go to school or work. If you want to go to university, then we will pay for you. My mother was very adamant about that. She said, 'No, education is the key.'

CAROLYN DOWSE

> My mother died when I was three and when my youngest sister was nine months. So one of our sisters raised my baby sister in New York, and another sister, Sadie Cartledge,

raised me. She was my mother. Education was big in our family. Our mother charged the older sisters to see to it that we received an education, because that was the way out of poverty.

Understandably, they made sure their children went to school *come hell or high water*. Becoming an educated black man or woman was an act of resistance. It was a viable way to fight and beat the system. Regardless if schools were segregated, with black schools being drastically inferior to white schools, Savannah's black community stuck together Umoja style and did whatever was necessary to ensure that its children were formally educated. Pastor Brown's father provided an excellent example of that togetherness.

PASTOR MATTHEW SOUTHALL BROWN, SR.

Christopher Frederick Brown, Big Chris, that was my daddy's name. He'd never drove a car in his life but rode a bicycle. Then he bought a car in 1941, a Plymouth, I won't forget. We went down to the riverfront to see it coming on the boat, and they had all that stuff on it to keep salt water, you know, from rusting it. I think that car cost 800-some dollars, brand new.

That car took my brother and two sisters, and Dr. Boston, who was a professor out of Savannah State. They were all going to Savannah State then. That car took one, two, three, four, five, six seven, that car took almost eight people to Savannah State every morning. Nine, with the driver. We had two benches put in on the side, inside the car. Two people in the front seat, two people sitting on both sides of the stool and four people on the backseat.

It's amazing what black people did, how do I want to put this, what black people did to make a living and to educate their children.

CAROLYN DOWSE

The school worked with the home. When I went from elementary to junior high, Beach Cuyler, nobody knew me and because I was so shy in those days they had like 7A1, 7A2, 3, 4, 5. 7A1 were the smart children and 7A5 would be the slow children. They put me in the slow class and I was very bored, but I said nothing. I went home everyday and cried and my sister went to the principal and she said, 'This child is very bright and she needs to be tested.' So they had me tested and then they skipped me a whole grade. And that's how I got in the top class, remained in the top class, made honor roll every six weeks. It's because the school and I had a teacher, Ella P. Law, who looked out for me. She would walk out the class and tell me I was in charge of the class. I would get so nervous, but they made me. And that's why I am the woman that I am today. Because the church, the school, and the home all worked together and molded me and shaped me and nurtured me.

MARY BUTLER SMITH

Mom started us at the Catholic school on East Broad Street in Kindergarten. We learned how to read. We learned what going to school was in Catholic Kindergarten. They didn't play with you. Those nuns had those switches off of trees; they were flexible. And they would tap you, and it would hurt. Shame on you, do the right thing.

White nuns, white fathers, all white. But they taught the children, taught 'em how to learn and retain. If you went to Catholic school, you were fixed for education for the rest of your life. That's why we were so good in school all the way through. We went through 'til about the fifth grade, and then

Mama switched us to black education. Could've been location for one thing. It could be that black-white thing. But anyhow, we went to the black schools and finished our education.

We had that solid education to begin with. Smarter than most other kids and that was just the truth. They just knew how to teach you, and you just had to learn. Now if you got ugly and they had to tap you with that switch, they would send you out of the classroom to—I don't wanna say the directory--the place where the father lived. And they would call your mom or dad or whatever, and they would come to pick you up. And Mom would take you home and give you a little shibby shabby talk or whatever.

When you got back, you acted like you had sense. You didn't play with the teacher. You learned. They didn't waste any time with you. You learned. That's why they turned out a lot of smart, black kids. They had the kernels in here [pointing to her head], but they knew how to bring it out. They knew how to bring out what you had in there. Unfortunately, you didn't always get that in the black instructors. You got a lot of loud talking and it was a different type of way they approached the education in teaching kids. They were rougher [stricter].

If you was smart, they didn't try to hold you back. They just had a different way of doing it. But you make it through if you had any courage at all to learn how to do what they asked you to do. Some marks on you, not literally, but marks inside. Hurt and like that, but you learned the lesson. Arithmetic and math was always my worst subjects. I didn't care that much for them, but I had to learn how to do them to a point. English and all that other stuff, I killed it. I loved it.

STEVEN WILLIAMS

Where Bartlett is now on Montgomery Crossroads is where Haven Home was then. Haven Home Industrial Training School. Once you get to Montgomery Crossroads, all that was dairyland. When you turn right on Abercorn and Bull, White Bluff Road, that was all dairyland. In fact, we got a marker put there. First, it was a boarding school for black girls. Then the board of education acquired it in 1934.

They had one graduation. Haven Home then went from the first grade to the twelfth. I had to transfer to Beach because they only went as high as tenth grade when I went. Can you imagine that? Knowing the same people and being in the same class with them from first to tenth grade. And it was discipline. Now this lady here, she was the principal. She was sort of like the judge and the teachers was like the bailiffs. They didn't need no security guards.

When I left Beach High School, I was ignorant. I finished high school, but I wasn't a high school student. I wasn't qualified. I played football and they just passed me on by. Playing football, you always hung with the dummies. Only dummies played football at that time. You got smart guys now. I remember we had, in my senior class, we had ten football players and a room full of dummies.

Mr. Steven Williams proved that education was not limited to a piece of paper. While a diploma was a passport into more opportunities, having it didn't mean that you could read and write proficiently enough to advance on the job. Upon realizing that his struggle to read and write would continue holding him back, Williams and a fellow service member taught themselves how to master the English language using a bible and a dictionary:

STEVEN WILLIAMS

I met a guy from Ohio, and me and him started talking. And he had the same story I had. So what we decided to do was get a bible and a dictionary and start learning. Start with the first word in each book. We went as far as we could go, starting from the first page. And anytime we would hear a new word, we would come back and try to find it in the dictionary. We did that to get an education that we missed in high school. It shows you what you can do when you ain't supposed to be able to do it. I got that education. I'm not smarter because of that. The more you learn, the dumber you are. You understand that? You realize how much you don't know. You really don't know nothing. But I was hungry for it. It ain't never too late.

CAROLYN DOWSE

I was studying one time, and I asked [my sister] how to spell something. She asked me, "Why do you think I have those dictionaries?" She provided encyclopedias too, The World Book, I'll never forget. But she would not just sit there and do my work or give me answers. I went to Columbia for my Master's in New York. I was able to go there and compete. I was able to go to University of Georgia, and I am an independent thinker. Everybody tells me I'm so much like her, because she was outspoken and she was also a principal.

The hunger for education dates back to the days of slavery. Susie King Taylor, the first black Army nurse, was illegally taught to read and write during slavery. Once emancipated, she opened her Savannah home as a school for former enslaved children and adults for a dollar a month. In her memoir,

Reminisces of My Life in Camp with the 33rd United States Colored Troops, she recalled having to turn students away because she could only handle 20 at a time. Further, "On March 25, 1865, the *Savannah Republican* noted the earnestness and avidity with which these liberated people seek information. Charles Coffin wrote that freedmen in Savannah were eager to obtain knowledge" (Perdue, 1973). And when 20 ministers sat down with General William Sherman to discuss the needs of African Americans post-slavery, next to land and money, education was high on the list.

White people had mixed feelings about black people being educated once freed. "Although education for Negroes was generally opposed by conservatives in North and South, some native whites in Savannah and the South in general accepted blacks as freedmen and urged that they be assisted in developing a school system—separate from whites, to be sure (Perdue, 1973)." A few of those whites, who might have very well been called abolitionists a few years prior, reasoned that blacks needed schools in order to educate themselves in their fight for justice and equality. However, "a few thought that freedmen should have access to education because, uninstructed and free, they would constitute a grave danger to society." Then others figured it was the best bet for them to acquire fundamentals in order to best be of service on their jobs.

The Freedmen's Bureau—federal agencies all over the South to assist in social welfare including building schools and hospitals—helped open several schools after the Civil War ended. One was the Beach Institute, located on E. Harris Street, in 1867. During the operation of those freedom schools, however, there were constant shortages of funds, books, supplies, and even classrooms. Fast forward to 1950 and those same complaints were still being made.

FLORRIE SCRIVEN

> We got the second-handed stuff or the third-handed or whatever handed down from them to us. So yeah, we wanted equal. Treat us equal like you do the others.

Black Savannah didn't wait on handouts or for some external body of people to turn their situation around. There are numerous accounts of us building our own. Take Carnegie Library, for instance.

In 1903, the City of Savannah partnered with the Georgia Historical Society to open up a library for white people. Three years later, 11 black businessmen put their money together to build one for black people. That first black library started off small, in a doctor's office on the corner of Price and Hartridge.

You'd go to a doctor's office, also black-owned, to borrow books that had been donated from members of the community.

In 1913, they applied for a grant to erect the beautiful Carnegie Library we see today. That wasn't an easy process though. The grant required proof of land ownership and matching funds. So the $12,000 they were approved for, they had to match.

Meanwhile, the white folks' library was still housed in one room of the Georgia Historical Society. They didn't have their own building until 1916, so Carnegie was actually Savannah's first public library. In 2017, Carnegie Library, located on the corner of Henry and East Broad, was recognized as one of Georgia's top 10 most beautiful libraries.

Carnegie was created for black people because they weren't allowed in white libraries. Middle class members of the black community masterminded and manifested what's still considered a jewel for the entire state. Building a facility that was equal to or even better than one that white people had built was no easy feat. The resources weren't comparable. That was certainly the case for many schools. Taxes were collected equally but distributed very unjustly, thereby affecting the quality of education for black students.

The separate but equal clause of 1896, which stated that states could allow segregation but the facilities between the races had to be of equal quality, was not being upheld at all. So in 1954, the Brown v. Board of Education ruling outlawed segregation in schools. A year later, after realizing that many southern states still weren't budging, the Supreme Court called for desegregation with deliberate speed. In 1964, 1.2 percent of African American students in the South attended school with whites. By 1968, the figures had risen to 32 percent (Kook, 2002). Carolyn Dowse remembers clearly when a fire was lit under Savannah's feet to integrate the schools.

CAROLYN DOWSE

> I was teaching at Moses Jackson when the lady from the state and the Director of Elementary Education came. They observed my class and they went back and told the personnel director, "We need her as a principal." They called me and said, "What would yo principal think if we took you from her?" I said, "I don't know." I said, "Number one, I have no courses in administration. I'm happy in the classroom." I was young and would get out there and play dodgeball with my little kids and all that and we loved each other. So they said, "Okay, we can get you some money to go to the University of Georgia." University of Georgia's graduate school had just integrated. That was in 1963. They paid for all my books. They paid for me to live in the dorm and everything. I had to take the NTE and the Miller's Analogy to qualify. I took it and passed it with flying colors. So I got in.
>
> I was completing my work in Athens and I got a call from the Board of Education. "We got a petition from the people in

the community and Hodge. They want us to send a strong black to Hodge because they are having lots of problems. So they said they want you to take Hodge." So I said, "I'll do what I can, but I can't promise you any miracles." I went there and I was supposed to have first through seventh [grades]. By the time I got there, the Supreme Court said you got to integrate the elementary school this year, like overnight. The superintendent called and said we got to integrate and the only way we can do it is to pair the schools. So they paired us with Hesse.

My background was in primary grades as a teacher, so they let me keep the primary grades and they bussed all of my upper grades to Hesse. I had to arrange to get all my upper grade books, chairs, everything to Hesse. And then one of the white parents told me, when they opened school, she said, "You seem to be so nice, so I want to tip you off. They planning to come and try to interrupt." So I said, okay. I called the Board, I said "I want county police." And I had county police all over. They were all up on the lawns, and I told the teachers, I said, "If anybody tries anything, they will be arrested because the kids are going to come in and we are all going to let them register."

Whites kept their kids out for six weeks. All on television: "I don't want my kids to go to that Hodge School." Reporters were out, the radio, everybody interviewing me. I said, "All is well. I'm fine." And it worked out. My brother was living then and he had retired as the first black supervisor at the post office. He got a job at the Y, just a little second job, and so he came over. "Sis, you alright?" I said, "You get on back on yo job." He looked and asked again. "Are you alright?" I said, "I'm fine. I can handle it."

Pastor Southall-Brown, my mentor, said, "When you are in an administrative position and you have people against you, you don't fight them. But you try to win them." So, what I did, I let them stay out there and grumble, and then all of them couldn't put their kids in private school because they didn't have the money. They needed to get their kids in school, so when they started softening up, I created a Beautification Day. I didn't need that, but I did and I used some our blacks along with them as leaders of the movement. They came over one Saturday and planted all these pretty little flowers. They became my best supporters, my class mothers. I let them be officers, integrated, and the PTA, they would come and run off work for the teachers. And that's how I got the schools integrated.

You'd think the signing of the Civil Rights Act of 1964 would've been black Savannah's moment of glory, its well-deserved opportunity to kick back, relax, and finally enjoy equal opportunity. But the back and forth of wins and losses persisted. To a large extent, they still do.

Soon after Judge Scarlett's decision to uphold school segregation and the Supreme Court's decision, the *Savannah Morning News* posed a question, asking its readers to consider if forced segregation was wrong then forced integration might be equally wrong. They questioned if school integration might be a form of discrimination. "If rights of one race are to be protected," they asked, "must we not also consider the rights of the other?" Considering that the nation, the state, and the city couldn't even get the separate but equal law right, the *Savannah Morning News* question wasn't even worth responding to.

As Gary Orfield, co-director at the Harvard Civil Rights Project, said best regarding to school integration, "The African-American struggle for desegregation did not arise because anyone believed that there was something magical about sitting next to whites in a classroom." It was because blacks recognized that without access to white schools, their children would always have the shorter end of the stick, having to use ragged textbooks passed down from the white schools, having to walk to school while white students rode buses, and sometimes having to end school early due to no air conditioning.

It wasn't until 1965 that the State Board of Education officially ended segregation in Savannah. While affluent white children were put into private schools, white children who weren't as well off were sent to public schools with black children and vice versa. Curt Williams shared a story of how a black teacher at Beach High School was mistreated during its years of integration.

CURT WILLIAMS

They had one of the most prejudiced woman over the school board, Dr. Martha Fay. That's when Beach first integrated, I think they had something like ten kids. One little white girl, she was best friends to the supervisor of the school, Dr. Martha Fay. And Irving, a black teacher, failed her. He say he wrote note after note for the parents. You can imagine what came out the white parents. "I ain't gon' talk to no nigga." So when he failed her, her friend showed the report to Dr. Fay, they was good friends. She came to the school, told him to leave the property, leave the campus. Irving was the type of guy, he bought a lot of the equipment that the school didn't have and put it in the classrooms. They didn't like that. Copy machine, all dat. They asked him to leave the classroom, get off the property. You cannot teach here anymore because you are, what's the word they used, incompetent or whatever.

So that's when the minister alliance heard about it. They took it up. You ever heard of Reverend Mitchell? Reverend Mitchell and the minister alliance took it up. They sued Dr. Fay. He got his job back, plus back pay. The hoe died with a heart attack. She got on the news and say, "I will go to jail before I put him back in the school system. I'm gonna bring my toothbrush and wash rag when I come to the meeting. If I have to go to jail, he will never teach in the public school system again." Those were her exact words. He still living. She gone. You ever heard God moves stumbling blocks out the way? She was a stumbling block.

With stories like this, I am reminded of Dr. Martin Luther King, Jr.'s rhetorical statement, "I fear I am integrating my people into a burning house." Was integration in the best interest of black people? Should we have fought harder in the direction of separate but equal? What would have been the difference in our communities had we had equal facilities and resources to our white counterparts, versus being forced to share physical spaces with them when we were unwanted?

---

1. Women were not allowed to vote until the passing of the 19th Amendment in 1920.

CHAPTER NINE

THE ROLE OF THE BLACK CHURCH

"I say y'all need to know all of that. Pass it on down." -Sadie Green

As Pastor Southall Brown Sr. said, the way we survived back then was with three things: each other, working hard, and prayer. Most black southerners have stories of being in church all day. Ms. Carolyn Dowse remembers it clearly.

CAROLYN DOWSE

> Besides school, church is all I know. On Sunday mornings, we had to clean our rooms, eat breakfast, wash up the dishes, and then you had to go to Sunday School. And we were active in the Sunday School, teaching and all that. Stayed for church and we were little ushers and all that. Then you went home and had a full-course meal. We didn't have television at all. So you sat around the table and she cooked on Saturday. Everything but the fried chicken. The potato salad, macaroni, and collard greens, the cakes and the pies, she did on Saturday. But the chicken was the only thing that couldn't be cooked early. And you always cooked a lot

because if you came by and your mother and your grandmother stopped by. Oh, Sister Mary, come on and join us. Everybody could eat. She made plenty. She cooked in these big pots like she was cooking for an army. And everything was from scratch. We sat around the table and we had family discussions and after that, you went back to BYPU [Baptist Young People's Union] and night service.

The black church played a central role in the African American struggle. Beginning in the sixteenth and seventeenth centuries, Catholic and Protestant churches took advantage of the burgeoning slave trade in West Africa and the invasion of the Americas. The earth-based traditional cultures and spiritual practices of African and Native American people were labeled witchcraft and devil worship and subsequently banned. Slaves were forbidden to practice their native religions and spiritual practices lest they be beaten, killed, or sold away from their loved ones.

The black church, when it was permitted, became a safe house for spiritual, religious, and communal sustenance for African Americans. It drew from African worship rituals including music, song, dance, and spirit possession (catching the Holy Ghost) and Christianity to create a unique system that gave black people mechanisms with which to heal and cope during and after slavery. Black churches were where the fightback lived, concealing a fierce resistance to slavery and discrimination, helping to organize and participate in slave rebellions, abolitionist meetings, and self-help societies. As local historian and Savannah State Africana Studies professor, Dr. Jamal Toure mentioned, "Once freedom was achieved in Savannah on December 21, 1865, it was the African ministers and businessmen/women who were the so-called radicals and militants." In some instances, the church functioned as a stop on the underground railroad to freedom.

The historic First African Baptist Church served as one of those stops for many enslaved persons. To this day, there are holes in the floorboards in certain areas of the church. If you weren't privy to the real reason for these holes arranged in a pattern that look like crosses set in a diamond, then you'd think they were for religious decoration. However, the holes provided fresh air for the enslaved refugees hiding beneath the floor, and the Nine Patch Quilt pattern on the ceiling of the church symbolized that it was a place of safety for runaway slaves.

After slavery, the power of the black church made it a target of white supremacists who turned the burning cross into a symbol of terror. Throughout the 1950s and 1960s civil rights era, hundreds of black churches were victims of gun violence and bombings. The 1963 bombing at the 16th Street Baptist Church in Birmingham, Alabama that killed four little girls is the most recognized instance, but it was far from the only one. Nevertheless, the black church, instead of allowing racists to destroy it, "practically willed itself to exponential growth through political self-determination, community outreach and organizing that made it, alongside historically black schools, lodges and civic groups, the most important Negro institution America has ever produced" (Joseph 2015).

The civil rights movement of the 1950s and '60s demonstrated the black church's fundamental role in our struggle for freedom and equality with black preachers such as Reverend Martin Luther King Jr. and Pastor Matthew Southall Brown Sr., and black churchwomen such as Mary McLeod Bethune and Amelia Boynton Robinson (born and educated in Savannah). These leaders became local and national figureheads of the era. Black churches were more than a place of worship, even locally, as was evident in W.W. Law holding weekly meetings at St. Philip A.M.E and Bolton Street Baptist Church.

FLORRIE SCRIVEN

We came up in First Nazareth Baptist. It was originated in Yamacraw in 1910. It was on St. Gall, and from St. Gall to Bryan and that was in 1945 when they built the Yamacraw Village and we had to move, so we moved in Frogtown at Berrien and Wilson. That church is still there. And then as our congregation grew, my pastor, W. Robinson, he started looking around for a place for us to build. So in 1943 we built at 44th and Hopkins near Beach High School. That's where we are now.

Our church supported the marches, undercoveredly. My pastor, the Reverend Robinson, admitted he was pastoring historical Bolton Street. Not First Nazareth, where we are now. He was pastoring Bolton Street at that time. He was the first pastor to allow them to have the NAACP meetings at his church. Most pastors refused at that time out of fear.

Black churches were more than places to worship and organize, though. They helped protect black communities against the ravages of poverty and white supremacy, educated black girls and boys, and gave black men and women a platform to speak and lead when society said "no." They provided a sense of self and a sense of place for their members. Along with the neighborhood you grew up in and the school you went to, the church was another village, representing religion, community, and home. The church was where you were christened at birth. It was where you were baptized and married. When you died, it was where you were memorialized. Next to the black woman, the late comedian and civil rights activist Dick Gregory named the black church as the second strongest force in America.

FLORRIE SCRIVEN

Church was a close-knit family too. Even the members themselves, just family. Real family. We ate together. We fellowshipped together. We were chastised together. They were able to chastise us. So if we needed it, it was no problem. Then we did the same thing with my children that came along and Lula Mae's children.

CAROLYN DOWSE

I had a terrible speech impediment, so I was very shy and introverted and my sister who raised me after our mother passed, along with the church, made me get up and speak. They made me. The women in the church looked out for us. They were an extension of the family, so we had the mothers at the home and we had the mothers in the church. So there was the church and the home and the school all working together, which we don't have today.

Church was not strictly religion. Church was also your family. I had a family in the church. Everybody says I'm so different today. I say, I never went to a speech therapist. I outgrew my shyness because the mothers in the church took me over. The elders took me over, and they worked with my sister. They worked with the home.

The church was not without fault though. I'd heard of the brown paper bag test before, where if you're darker than the bag, then you were considered too dark to enter a particular church building or organization. I knew that some fraternities, sororities, and nightclubs checked skin tones, but I had no clue that some churches operated that way too.

STEVEN WILLIAMS

Matter of fact, we got a famous church in Savannah over there on Habersham and Taylor. It's next to the high rise over there. St. Joseph's used to be over there at one time. It's called First Congregational Church. He [pointing to Darrien sitting next to me] could go one Sunday and not get in because he's too black. The church. You had to be light skinned like you to get in. Brown stick around; black get back. It's a white, pretty church, sitting by the square. I think it's an independent church because they didn't associate with other churches. There were several churches like that.

CAROLYN DOWSE

There was discrimination between the light skinned blacks and the dark skinned blacks. There was St. Matthew's for the light-skinned, and St. Stephen's for the dark-skinned. Those are Episcopal church. On Jefferson Street, there was a St. Stephen's Episcopal. My girlfriend was dark, so she had to go there. The light-skinned Episcopalians went to St. Matthews. I have lived to see it all.

Sexism was another issue in the black church. Ms. Dowse, also an ordained minister, has had her fair share of struggle.

CAROLYN DOWSE

When I went to join the Savannah Baptist Minister's Union, I told Pastor Brown what I was gonna do, he said, "I won't be there to support you." And when the president came down, he said, "We're so glad to have Reverend Dowse as a visitor." I said, "Thank you for welcoming me, but I did not come as a visitor. I came to apply for membership." They started a whole discussion on me as if I was not in the room, and they talked and talked about females and everything. I sat there and said nothing. They finally got a vote through to admit me.

She later became the first female vice president of the Savannah Baptist Minister's Association. "Anytime you're first, you get kicked." For the city of Savannah, Ms. Dowse claimed a lot of firsts within the educational circles and the religious circles: first black to serve on the Southern Association of Colleges and Schools, first female licensed in the history of St. John's Baptist Church, and the first female minister accepted in the Savannah Baptist Minister's Association. It wasn't without struggle though, and the strife wasn't just behind the scenes. It was also smack dab in front of the congregation. From trying to join the minister's association to trying to preach, Ms. Dowse emphasized how difficult it was being a black female preacher back in those days.

CAROLYN DOWSE

I went to this particular church. I was invited to preach. I got there, and I always go early, and I sat in the audience and the pastor invited me back in his office. He started all of this about, "You know what the bible says about females." I said, "So, what are you trying to say?" He said, "You will not be able to go in the pulpit." I said, "Did you know before I got there that I was a female? Why didn't you let me know?" Now I always wore a robe, because I used to wear these real fancy clothes and fancy hats. There was a minister who did that, and I realized that I didn't wanna be like that because you look at the person and what they're wearing and not the message. I said, "What about my robe? Can I put that on?" He said, "No, and you can't go in the pulpit." I said, "Thank you. I will preach from the floor and I will not put my robe on."

I went out there and saw this lady, Queenie Coleman, she's now deceased. I said, "Queenie, let's go in the back to the restroom and pray." I told her what I was up against and we prayed. I went out and sat on the front pew, and this elderly lady in the back—Oh God, I got chills going through me—when she saw me, she said, "Oh, no. We not going to have this today." I said, "All is well." I went to her and I hugged her. I said, "Please, let's have no commotion. I'm here to bring a message. If somebody gets saved, it doesn't matter if it's from the floor. I am fine."

Women make up more than half of churches' memberships, yet less than a third of leadership positions. That doesn't add up. There's one church in particular, the United House of Prayer, that is more known for cooking up plates of oxtails, turkey wings, macaroni, and red rice than for its unusual practices, unorthodox leaders, and keeping its women tucked in the shadows.

SWEET DADDY GRACE'S UNITED HOUSE OF PRAYER

Across the nation, there are over 145 United House of Prayer churches. The organization has deep roots here in Savannah, with its first building dating back to the 1880s. Bishop Charles Manuel Grace, better known as Sweet Daddy Grace, was the organization's first bishop. He visited Savannah a few a year, and each time the congregation would put on a colorful parade for him. *Drums and Shadows* described his entrance into the church being announced by a sharp whistle to cease all mouths and movements. "The Armor Bearers leave the building to escort the Bishop to his seat of honor. Soon they return, followed by the Queen who is arrayed in a pale green satin evening dress over which is worn a black velvet cape lined with scarlet. A double line of uniformed guards follows, and marching proudly between the lines is the Bishop" (p. 47).

Daddy Grace passed away in 1960, but his legacy lives on in Savannah. The United House of Prayer is no *once upon a time* establishment in this city. There are now four locations—on Ogeechee Road, on West Bay, on West Victory, and on Sixth Street. Savannah has hundreds of churches, but you can recognize a House of Prayer by the massive concrete lions sitting on each side of the staircase leading to the front door. Daddy Grace's name spurred reactions in everyone. They either chuckled, smirked, or raised their eyebrows and puckered their lips followed by an "Oooh, child...."

MATILDA "PATT" BROWN

I was sort of raised up in the House of Prayer. It was a little shack on 34th Street. They used to have on the third Sunday in September convocation Sunday. They had all kind of big things going on. It was sawdust on the flo.' They didn't have no real flooring.

JOHNNIE PARRISH

They was in a sawmill where they used to cut lumber. It was a warehouse. They put sawdust so it wouldn't raise so much dirt when they run by there and take them hundred dollar bills. We used to go there every year.

MATILDA "PATT" BROWN

She didn't have so much, but she made all kind of sacrifices in that church. By your beliefs, you shall be saved. I know my grandma in heaven. The people truly believed in Sweet Daddy Grace.

RUBY JONES

They said he was God and all kind of stuff like that.

JOHNNIE PARRISH

They used to see which church was gon' give 'em the most. See, he had all them girls with them evening gowns, pretty girls. He had them fingernails all out there. And he used to call 'em fools and all that stuff. But see, Daddy Grace didn't do nothing for them people. Now McCollough, the one that did all that stuff, when he took over after Daddy Grace died, McCollough built all them nice churches. McCollough did that. Now Walker did some of it too. Daddy Grace just used to come in town to collect every year.

I visited House of Prayer about ten years ago and the then bishop was also called Daddy. Hearing him being called Daddy shocked and confused me. Even those who weren't members of the churched called him Daddy Grace. When I relocated to Washington, D.C., where the church is headquartered, I asked several locals what they knew about the church. "You talking about Daddy Grace?" I was thrown off about it until I heard my eldest elder yet speak on it.

LAURA LANGLEY, 99 YEARS OLD

Don't nobody say nothing about them Catholics calling the priest father.

There are several things that Daddy Grace is known for—his long hair and fingernails, the bountiful tithes and offerings he collected, the loyalty of his followers, and his church's band and parades.

MATILDA "PATT" BROWN

The parade, it used to *really* be a parade.

JOHNNIE PARRISH

They had a parade though. They got one of the best bands you wanna see in this town.

MARY BUTLER SMITH

We used to go up to House of Prayer as kids, and we'd sneak in. We'd go to dance to the music, and they'd put our behinds out of there.

CAROLYN DOWSE

As children, we used to laugh. Oh, Jesus. I mean they had sawdust and people all down in the sawdust. We were little children, and we used to go there sometimes just to be curious. They would tell us how the people did when he walked in and all of that. Sweet Daddy Grace. He had this long, flowing hair. And when they had their convocation and the parade, you couldn't get from the east to the westside.

FLORRIE SCRIVEN

My sister was just talking about that band. In fact, when my mom deceased and we had her homegoing service, my sister went and got the trumpet player to play her favorite song, which was "Sending Up My Timber."

The United House of Prayer is actually honored in the Smithsonian for its music. And while there are many things that have been said and can be said about a man who wore long painted fingernails and left this world having amassed over 25 million dollars, no one can deny his influence.

There were many myths about Marcelino Manuel da Graça, better known as Sweet Daddy Grace and also known as Bishop Charles Manuel Grace. Two of the most infamous untruths were that he sold seats to heaven and bricks to the stairway to heaven. There were testimonies that his followers swore by that non-followers refused to believe—like how he'd heal the ill and injured just by laying a hand on them.

There were sides and stories to Daddy Grace that many people still don't know about. Many faces frown at the fact that he accumulated so much property, but they don't know that most of it belongs to the church. They don't know how many people have thanked him for shelter and a lending hand to help make ends meet. When a number of black churches were implementing brown-paper bag tests, Bishop Grace accepted everyone regardless of class, complexion or denomination. And a fond memory of Pastor Southall Brown Sr.'s affirmed that Daddy Grace also used his power for the people:

PASTOR MATTHEW SOUTHALL BROWN, SR.

When Negroes received their franchise, their right to

vote, and we were trying to get as many black folks to register, Philip Cooper, my wife's biology teacher over at Beach, took the class down to the Registrar's Office. That's how we got a lot of people on the books. So I decided since that Daddy Grace leading all these people, I'ma get him involved. So I wrote him a letter and I told him about the struggle and Martin Luther King and now that we have a right to vote, I'm asking you if you would get all of your constituents, your parishioners, tell them to go down and register to vote.

He got the letter, and know how I know he got the letter? Because the morning news, a few days later, had that influx of Negroes packed the registrar's office, and it couldn't have been nobody else and as a result of that letter that I wrote him. All he had to do was tell 'em, and they'd do it. They didn't question the source or nothing.

When Daddy Grace died, his body made a seven-city tour before finally arriving in New Bedford, New York, where he had originally immigrated to in 1903 from the Island of Brava, Cape Verde and was buried in 1960. At times, there would be more than 500 cars in the funeral motorcade and more than 700 people packed into the church for the funeral service. About 5,000 followers were at the cemetery for his burial.

CHAPTER TEN

MIGRATIONS AND ENLISTMENTS

> *"Most people didn't want their children and grandchildren to know about the old days. They just wanted them to have a better life."* - Madie Underwood

For some, no matter how hard they worked or prayed or stuck together, it wasn't enough. As a result of the smothering hand of racism, many African Americans across the South left the grounds that they, their parents, and grandparents had been born and raised on. Similar to the days of slavery, the North seemed to be the promised land. In *The Warmth of Other Suns*, Isabel Wilkerson wrote:

> From the early years of the twentieth century to well past its middle age, nearly every black family in the American South, which meant nearly every black family in America, had a decision to make. There were sharecroppers losing at settlement. Typists wanting to work in an office. Yard boys scared that a single gesture near the planter's wife could leave them hanging from an oak tree. They were all stuck in a caste system as hard and unyielding as the red Georgia clay, and they each had a decision before them. In this, they were not

unlike anyone who ever longed to cross the Atlantic or the Rio Grande.

Although they didn't know it then, they were part of what is now referred to as the Great Migration, when over six million black folks moved from the South to the North, West, and Midwest seeking better education, more opportunities for employment, desegregation, and respect—to be called miss, missus, and mister, like their white counterparts, and not "gal" or "boy." The city you ended up in usually depended on your city's train route. Whereas many from Louisiana went to California, Ohio, and Illinois, most Georgians went to Philadelphia, New Jersey, and New York.

STEVEN WILLIAMS

Going to New York was the thing to do. The people that migrated up north when I was a kid, we didn't lose contact with those people. During that time, a boy was expected to leave home at 18. We wanted to leave, because we saw the struggles of our parents. They was catching hell trying to raise us.

MARY BUTLER SMITH

A lot of our family had gone up North already. Mom didn't talk much, period, but Daddy knew the reason I wanted to go. I wanted more for myself. So they put me on a train.

RUBY JONES

I trained at Veteran Hospital in New York. See, I lived in

New York a long time. In New York, there's a school for everything. If you want to be a butcher to cut meat, there's a school. If you want to be an artist, there's a school. If you want to do hair, there's a school. New York got 910 different schools. Anything you wanna learn, they got a school for it. That's why my husband said he wanted to go there. My daughter wanted to learn childcare.

I have another sister that's a nurse too. When we all finished school, we all went North. My husband wanted to go up north. He said it would be better for the kids. I said I didn't know, but I went. I had to learn it. It was busy, and I like to be busy. But people don't talk to you. They don't speak to you. You take care of yo business and I'll take care of mine. You live in a building. You live upstairs and they live downstairs. You come out and they won't say nothing to you. But if you in trouble, they'll help you. Other than that, just talking to you, no.

I lived in Manhattan. They called that The Jungle. Manhattan had everything going on. A lot of movies there. 42nd Street.

Everybody moved up north to make more money, but you still had to spend it because things cost mo. I came back here because my mother left me a house on West 39th Street.

MADIE UNDERWOOD

I had to make some moves so that I could get settled and where I could get settled better, meaning getting a place where I could relax and function in and make a good living for my kids.

They still had prejudices going on right here in Philadelphia. Back then, we had the understanding there was no prejudice up north, and that's what we thought. But when we got here, we found out that was not true.

Not everyone found what they were looking for. As Maya Angelou wrote, "The climate which the immigrants imagined as free of racial prejudice was found to be discriminatory in ways different from the Southern modes and possibly even more humiliating." Angelou didn't elaborate on why northern discrimination was more humiliating, but if I had to guess, I'd paint a picture instead. In the south, black people knew what to expect. They could pretty much accurately predict that they would be judged and/or denied on the basis of their skin color. It was the belief, however, that things were different in the north. Justice, equality, and opportunity existed above the Mason Dixon line.

So, for example, you use your financial gains to move your black family into the predominately white suburbs where the houses are sturdier, the crime is lower, and the schools have better resources and reputations. Excitedly, you throw a housewarming party and even invite a few neighbors over. Two days into your living there, a letter from the neighborhood association is on your front door asking you to respect the peace of the place and strongly consider their offer to purchase your newly purchased home. Here are some of the stories of disappointment.

STEVEN WILLIAMS

> The North represented, in my mind and many black folk, a better place to live. Better opportunities. But it wasn't all that much. They was segregated just like we was down here, almost. You could get a job, if they satisfied the white people first. So it was still segregated. It didn't make a difference. But you had to manage because it was an opportunity. It was better than it was here.

MARY BUTLER SMITH

I remember working for the Philadelphia naval shipyard and they signaled they were going to close. I put in an application for a job in New York, and that's when I left Philadelphia and went to New York. I got a job with the federal government. It was a good job. I was a secretary and then I got promoted and worked as supervisor.

Many of my employees were white and would give me a hard time because of that. I would go in the bathroom to shed some of my tears because I couldn't hit some of them crackas in the head like I wanted to for the way they were treating me. The company was just initiating typewriters. I had to learn how to use 'em then teach them how to use 'em. And they would do everything they could to make me look bad. And I was determined not to retaliate.

While I was in my shipyard, my supervisor, a white man, called me over and said, "Ms. Butler, can I ask you a question?" I said, "You the boss." He asked if I had a problem with any of the women working under me. "I do," I told him. "And I think you know what that's all about." I threw the ball in his corner, and he said, "Yes, I do. But as far as your performance, I'm impressed. That's why you're working here. And I like the way you're carrying yourself as a supervisor, so as far as I'm concerned, you aren't doing anything wrong. You're doing everything right. The fault is with them. Keep on doing what you're doing." Once I had set my feet in my concrete, I didn't get nasty. I just got firmer.

For some, going from one state to another wasn't far enough. The problem wasn't just the South or the North; it was the country as a whole. Some went "back to Africa," as Marcus Garvey named the movement in the 1920s. Civil rights leaders and Pan-African revolutionaries, Stokely Carmichael (who later changed his named to Kwame Toure) and W.E.B. Du Bois, respectively, moved to West Africa in the '60s. Poet and author, Maya Angelou did too, as did civil rights activist and singer, Nina Simone, who moved to Liberia in the '70s.

Even more moved to Europe. While it might seem odd that black people would flee problems created by white people in their own country to go to another country that's overwhelmingly white, many black expatriates found refuge in countries like the U.K. and France. It was an interesting exchange though. Traditionally, Europeans had left Europe for the U.S. in search of the opportunities and freedom that the country boasted. Yet, you had native Americans—black Americans—leaving the States for Europe in search of those same opportunities and freedoms.

> The African-American community in postwar Paris included painters, jazz musicians, novelists and journalists, and it may have numbered about 500 persons in the years around 1950. Its most famous public figures were the celebrated performer Josephine Baker and the much-acclaimed author Richard Wright, but Paris also became the refuge for many other black Americans who sought to escape from American racial prejudices in the streets, cafés and hotels of the French capital (Kramer 2001).

Mr. Omar Boone was one such expat. He was born in New Jersey and now lives in Savannah, but in between, he's spent a good deal of time in Europe, where he developed his artistry in painting, sculpting, and producing art. I first met him about five or so years before I interviewed him. I was walking into the Bull Street Library and he was walking past it with his now 16-year-old Lhasa Apso. I can't recall exactly what was said, but he started simple conversation with me that turned into about a ten minute chat about Savannah and Savannah College of Art and Design (SCAD) and his world travels. He was so lively and full of smiles and stories in his dark shades. Before going our separate ways, he handed me his black, lime green lettered business card. By the time I called him, five years later, he didn't remember me, but he was still unabashedly ready to share his story.

OMAR BOONE, 88 YEARS OLD

When I was 22 years old, a friend of mine and his wife were living in Switzerland. He started in America while his wife was in school in Switzerland. He told me, "She's in school in Switzerland and I'll be working in Germany. And it's so much inexpensive to go to school to Europe than it is here in New York." I was going to the city college in New York, then I transferred to the University of Geneva in Switzerland for about a year and a half, then I dropped out because I had to learn French in all of my classes. That's how I happened to go to Europe. I stayed for years over there.

I was able to support myself because I have this voice that I was able to dub over Italian westerns. In Paris, I used to dub an awful lot of films. So that's what kept me going for all the years I lived in Europe. When I come back from Europe, I got to be very well known in Italy, as well as in London. I had my first exhibition in London in a Bond Street gallery. That's how it started me as an artist.

I asked him what it was like once he'd settled good in Europe.

OMAR BOONE

I was like a god on Mt. Olympus in Greece, and I had the world at my feet. I knew James Baldwin. We used to hang out at the same cafe in Paris where a lot of the expatriates and a lot of the jazz musicians who would come to Europe and wouldn't want to go back to the United States once they saw how good it was over there. And we all were expatriates there in Paris. James Baldwin. Chester Himes. Gordon—I forget his name, the saxophone player. But we all congregated in Paris. We were treated as…humans. And this is going back to the '50s. I just felt like a human. I had more beautiful women than a man could want. They loved that brown skin.

On why in the world he would want to come back to the States after being treated like a god overseas, he said:

OMAR BOONE

I'm a gypsy. That's what I am. When I came back to the United States in '74 or '75, I was back out to L.A. and I stayed in L.A. from about to '75 until about '85. Yeah, it was about 10 years and that was the second time I'd lived in L.A. and I came back to the east coast and my mother passed in 1995. Then, after my mother died, I stayed on and I went to upstate New York. That's where I stayed and bought property up there.

Next, I wanted to know why Savannah. Of all the places in the world he's lived and visited, why did he decide to lay his hat in the C-Port?

OMAR BOONE

I moved to Savannah in 2006, but I came here in 2005 when my surrogate daughter said that she was living here in Savannah and that I should come. I said, "You must be out of your fucking mind." Being a northerner, the impression of the South was full of prejudice. I thought of the civil rights movement, and all of that was in the back of my head. I would have never thought of coming to Savannah. She said, "Omar, come down here and see." That was in 2005. I came down here and spent a week. She introduced me to some of her friends, and I got to know a few people, and I thought, "This is beautiful." It was so similar to where I was living then in Berkshire; there was a lot of old New England money up there. I decided to put my place up for sale. I sold my place in 2006, and I made a killing on my property in upstate New York, and I brought it all down to Savannah in 2006. And I've been here ever since.

I've been to many many places, and the houses here were number one. I thought that the downtown particularly had an elegance about it. I was used to being in that type of environment wherever I've lived in the world. I've lived in places that were comfortable for me, and Savannah is very comfortable for me.

Omar and other black expatriates moving and living abroad represented a very small percentage of black migrants during the civil rights era, but the impact they made cannot be denied. Nor can that of those who left the South for the North, Midwest, and West, about six million over the course of sixty years. That was a major shift, a huge turning point. Leaving your homeland, what's most familiar to you, is never easy, but it's always an option. To be free is to have options. The more options you have, the freer you are, and the less disrespect you're more apt to accept. Like an abused spouse who leaves their abuser, the power funnels from the abuser to the survivor. And like an abused spouse trying to leave, the abuser won't always allow for an easy escape. Isabel Wilkerson researched realities black folk faced when trying to flee various cities throughout the South.

> When the people kept leaving, the South resorted to coercion...Those trying to leave were rendered fugitives by definition and could not be certain they would be able to make it out. In Brookhaven, Mississippi, authorities stopped a train with fifty colored migrants on it and sidetracked it for three days. In Albany, Georgia, the police tore up the tickets of colored passengers as they stood waiting to board, dashing their hopes of escape. A minister in South Carolina, having seen his parishioners off, was arrested at the station on the charge of helping colored people get out. In Savannah, Georgia, the police arrested every colored person at the station regardless of where he or she was going. In Summit, Mississippi, authorities simply closed the ticket office and did not let northbound trains stop for the colored people waiting to get on (163).

If there's one thing that black people are good at—or any oppressed people, for that matter—it's making a way out of no way. Telling someone they can't leave only makes the idea of the promised land that much sweeter, and imagination precedes actualization. Once our minds were made to leave, we left. And like Albert in *The Color Purple* after Celie hightailed out of his life, the South was hit hard by the absence of over 6 million people over the course of 60 years.

Through the Great Migration, black southerners transformed urban America and recasted the social and political order of every city they touched, forcing the South to search its soul and finally lay aside a feudal caste system (Wilkerson, 9).

ENLISTMENTS

African Americans have fought for this country throughout its history, defending and serving a country that in turn denied them their basic rights as citizens. African-American soldiers played a substantial role from the American Revolutionary War to the War in Vietnam (and on through the wars in Iraq and Afghanistan) although they were subjected to legal segregation and discrimination in the military. Until the mid-20th century, African-American soldiers did not even receive their due recognition.

The beginning of the 20th century was marked by World War I, and thousands of black men registered for the draft in hopes of earning greater rights at home. Despite high enlistment rates and their desire to serve on the front lines, white military leaders believed African Americans were not physically, mentally, or morally capable of surviving warfare and were subsequently downgraded to positions that required more muscle than brain.

PASTOR MATTHEW SOUTHALL BROWN SR.

All quartermasters had was menial jobs—stacking gas, driving trucks, cooking. If you wanted to join the infantry to close the gap, and we did, there was something like, ten, fifteen thousand black soldiers who signed up, but they did not accept but 2,221. I was one of them—young, crazy, looking for action.

CURT WILLIAMS

We didn't have no important jobs. Even with the navy, when they first begin to let blacks go in the navy and the air force, that was one of the last branches that they let blacks get into, but when we first went in, only thing they would have us doing is cleaning the deck and working in the kitchen.

In the face of these limitations, notable contributions were made to war efforts, including the remarkable work of the 369th Infantry Regiment, also known as the "Harlem Hellfighters," who were awarded with France's highest military award for successfully front-lining combat for more than six months without losing any prisoners or territory (having received less training than any other unit). Although black soldiers had proven themselves time and time again, leading up to and during World War II, the U.S. military maintained that African Americans were not as capable as white soldiers. Still, more than a million black soldiers volunteered to serve in the Armed Forces in the fight against the Nazis.

World War II was a breakpoint for apartheid within the Armed Forces, and it marked the beginning of the end for racial separation. In 1948, President Harry S. Truman issued

Executive Order 9981, which abolished military segregation and required equal treatment and opportunity without regard to race, color, religion or national origin. Actual reform was slow, however, as seems to be the case with most change in America, and it wasn't until five years later that segregation officially ended for all military units. By the time the Korean War started in 1950, black soldiers served in all combat operations.

The Vietnam War had the most African Americans ever to serve in an American war. Since then, enlistment rates have continuously risen. As former Savannah mayor Otis Johnson wrote in his memoir, *From "N Word" to Mr. Mayor*, "The career options available for a young black male high school graduate in 1960 were to go college, get a job, or join a branch of the military." Since Johnson's family couldn't afford to send him to college, he decided on the U.S. Navy. Four of my grandmother's five sons chose the military as well, one for each branch except the Coast Guard. In 2015, black soldiers "made up 19% of the [Department of Defense] active-duty military— somewhat higher than their share of the U.S. population ages 18 to 44 (13%)" (Parker, Cilluffo, and Stepler 2017).

STEVEN WILLIAMS

I spent eight years in the Air Force and loved it. The service was a lifesaver for black boys. That was the place to go. That was one of the best decisions I'd ever made when I went in the service. I was 18. Well, I left Savannah when I was 18. I used to go to New York every summer when I was 16 and 17 to work for the summer. I went to New York when I graduated high school and I didn't like the way things was going. It was the same thing all over again: minimum wages. Of course, I didn't have no skills. I was ignorant. I got a high school diploma, but I didn't have the education to go along with it. But anyway, I joined the Air Force after I was in New York for about six months. That's the best thing that ever happened to me. I remember when I first went in the Air Force, I came to the conclusion that now I got my own wardrobe, because you couldn't own your own clothes.

The Air Force was segregated. Everything was. You go to New York and you ride next to a white person, but it was still segregated. You know you wasn't wanted. The service was a different kind of segregation. You sleep in the same barracks with 'em, same room, share the same bathroom with 'em. You laugh and talk and shoot pool and gamble and do everything else together. It was almost like kinfolks or something like that, but once they got out the gate, it was back to what it was. It came on you so fast. They acted like they didn't know who you was. If they saw you in town, or something like that, they didn't speak to you. Same business as usual. But once we got on the base, we was all buddy buddy.

Wasn't too many black officers. Once in a while you might see one, and it'd make us proud to see 'em. You had your limitations with how far you could go up the ladder. And that's one thing I was disgusted about. It's disappointing when you know you deserve to make something, make another rank, progress, and you know these people holding you back because you black. It sort of did something to me and I started drinking a lot. I became a drunk. At eighteen and nineteen years old, I was living in a foreign country. Stayed in Japan two years, living in a hotel in downtown Tokyo. At that age, I was exposed to a lot of stuff that really ruined me. Everything was cheap. Prostitution was legal over there. Getting drunk was cheap. That was really something. I don't think too many people really thought about it like that. It was something that really got my attention. This was a different world. I still think about it sometimes.

I was drunk for 12 years, and I had reached that point where it was a point of no return. There's a point in everybody's life where there's no return. You in it and that's it. And it had got to the point where I was drunk every day. Waking up in the morning searching for a drink, you know, without money. That was a struggle. I got out the military because it became a problem, me drinking. I knew that sooner or later I was going to do something that was going to cause me to get a bad discharge, a bad record.

CURT WILLIAMS

We wa'nt nothing but a target, a human shield. That Vietnam War was to cut down on the population. Think about it. They didn't have no goal. They didn't have no Ivory like France took off Africa, you know. That's why that's theirs now. They didn't have no oil fields. Why were we over there? They cannot answer that question. Only way was to bring down the population 'cause all the guys that went with me, I haven't seen them any of 'em since the last patrol we went on. I'll never forget that, but I don't like to talk about it. What were we over there fuh? They can't tell you themselves. Because of the population. It was too many of us and we was the ones that they was drafting back in them times. We didn't volunteer. We was told to report down to yo post office on such and such day 'cause you are going in the service.

I had 'bout three friends had high ranking. I'll never forget that. They came up with different tesses [tests] that they gave us. They knew we wa'nt gon pass them tesses. We, black men, it's hard for us to pass a test. That's a known fact. I don't care how smart you are, when they give you that test. You had to start off from the chain of command from yo city official all way up to yo federal government. Who knew all that stuff? We didn't know all that stuff! So, you got the pink slip. That's what they did to our black G.I.s when they seen some of 'em major and colonel and all that. These brothers is staying in longer, then they retire from us in 20 years then they can go and work on a job for 20 years.

They living in the same kinda house I'm living in. We got to cut this out. So they start giving us tesses. You got too much stomach. PT. If you can't pass it, you out of the service back then in the '60s. That's what they did to us. And we don' serve for dem and got kilt for dem.

My boy got 50% of his stomach blowed out in a tank division. Two years ago, he don' been out over 50 something years, they just start giving him his benefits. But he went down to Beach, he taught down there and don' retired. Now he sitting on easy street. That's what they don't like. Now they got to pay him, although he up in age now. He 74 or something like that, and they got to pay him for the rest of his life. But look how long it took.

When we first got out, I remember I came from Seattle, Washington. We all got down and kissed the ground, but the old protestors was calling us baby killas. We had to do what we was told there. 'Private William, we going through this, no prisoners. Destroy 'em.' That was our job. If we didn't do what Kelly dem told us to do, what they was gonna do? Co'rt Martial us? Kick us out the service or put us in the stockade. But they looked at us, these stupid individuals. They didn't know anything about the military, so they didn't actually know how the military worked. You see where I'm coming from?

When we got out and came back home to our hometown, our state representative had supposed to call all veterans and discharged veterans, and counsel us and tell us our benefits for buying homes and this that, how you keep your insurance up with one dollar a month then after 20 years you get full benefits. We didn't know none of this. I'll never forget, a girl name Gloria. I went by the VA to buy my first home. I'll never forget this long as I live. She saw me, "Oh, Mr. Curtis. Welcome back. You came in to collect on yo insurance?" I said what insurance? Not only me, thousands of us didn't know nothing about it.

Back in 1942, though, when most of the GIs was getting out the service after the war, in every major city, they built project houses for us. San Francisco and Oakland, they had a place called Tin City. I went there and visited. I mean, the house was made of nothing but tin. Shacks. But Carver Village? They put lil block houses out there. $12 a month for 30 years. A lot of them houses still standing out there in Carver Village. All them lil' ole small block houses? Them houses was built in 1942 for the black GIs. The government owned them and you wa'nt renting 'em out, you was buying 'em. One thing 'bout them lil' houses out there, you had plenty front yard and you had plenty backyard and a lot of the original ones dead and left it or they sold out, and people have enlarge 'em.

PASTOR MATTHEW SOUTHALL BROWN, SR.

In my family, there are four generations of men who fought to protect this nation. My daddy was World War 1, I was World War II, my son was Desert Storm, and his son was Iraqi Freedom. When I was 17, I got my high school diploma in this hand and I got my orders with the military in this hand.

When I got out of the military, Union Bag[1] was already open. I went out there to get me a job and the man told me he had a job for me on the woodpile. You know, they make paper out of wood. So I told him I said, 'Well according to what they told us in the military, we're supposed to get a job comparable to what we were doing in the military.' Excuse the expression, that cracker looked at me and he told me, he said, 'boy, we give you what we want you to have.' That was back in 1947.

I looked at him and I told him, I said, 'Sir, I fought. I landed on Normandy D plus five, with the outfit flying balloons.' I said, 'Later, in 1944 when Hitler made his infamous breakthrough and they didn't have any boys or soldiers that looked like you to close the gap,' I said, 'and the general sent an edict down to all quartermaster units, black units, to say that if you want to join the infantry all you had to do was sign up. Over 10,000 signed up, but they took only 2,221 and I was one of the 2,000.' I said, 'I crossed the Elbe River and fought across the Rhine into Berlin and waited on the Russians.' I said, 'And you telling me boy you take?' I said, 'I feel like knocking you into next week.' By that time, that cracker was trembling, 'Well, we sho appreciate what you boys did.'

The 2,221 of World War II were a group of black men who had answered the U.S. Army's call for volunteers to replace the 23,000 white infantrymen who were either killed or too badly hurt to rejoin combat during the Battle of the Bulge in Germany in 1944. Few black soldiers had been allowed to join combat units before then, but the Army really had no choice at that point, so they urged soldiers in "noncombat jobs to volunteer for infantry duty" (Vogel 2000). Soldiers of all races and backgrounds signed up, but black soldiers were forced to demote their rank so as not to outrank the white infantrymen.

Sadly, though not surprisingly, "a lot of [the black volunteers] never got their rank back" (Vogel 2000). Equally unfortunate was the fact that despite these black men volunteering for combat, risking their lives, and surrendering their rank for the cause, they returned home to a country that refused to treat them as equals. Further, many black soldiers—and not just the 2, 221 but most during and prior to the Korean War—died before they ever, if ever, received recognition for their contributions to America's war efforts[2]. Not even on screen. As Curt said best, "When they make dem movies, they don't even give us no roles to play."

---

1. Union Bag and Paper, a paper mill, merged with Camp Manufacturing in 1956, forming Union Camp. In 1999, Union Camp was purchased by International Paper, which still stands today on West Lathrop Avenue.
2. I was sitting in Washington National Airport in D.C. when I saw Pastor Brown on the television. In August of 2019, Pastor Matthew Southall Brown, Sr. was invited to commemorate 32 fellow black volunteer infantry men buried in the Netherlands.

CONCLUSION

"Y'all better get it together because I'm not gon' live forever." – Sadie Green

The stories and research in this book isn't just the history of the interviewed elders. It's black Savannah's history. It's Savannah's history. It's Georgia's history. It's the history of this nation. It's all black people's history and it's also the history of all human beings. It's an intricate quilt of experiences and memories. But it's also wildly complex, as history is. There isn't just one side to it nor is there is an absolute conclusion. Dr. Mark Carnes, Professor of History at Barnard College, said it best: "The complexity of the past renders it nearly incomprehensible and its subjectivity mocks all who propose tidy conclusions." History is cyclic, repeating itself with new characters and sometimes, but not always, new circumstances too.

Savannah is not peripheral to history's beauty and complexity. It's central to it in so many ways. I remember being blown away learning that the largest slave sale in American history, the Weeping Time, happened right here in Savannah. I also recall the "wow" that passed my lips when I learned that the famous 40 acres and a mule agreement was made in Savannah. I held the same awe when I realized First African Baptist was actually the first of its kind in the United States. Like, there are so many Baptist churches claiming to be the first in its name, yet Savannah has the actual first one. That still blows my mind.

It's in the blood. It's not coincidence. When people visit New Orleans for the first time they often mention the vibes of the city. They can feel the spirit of the ancestors heavy. It's as if they can still hear the drums and the cries, the celebrations and the mourning. It's still there. The same goes for Savannah. It might be packaged as a ghost tour, but the spirits are indeed still present. The stories are still making their way down. You would think those memories are forbidden, like they don't have as much right to exist as the tallest statutes in the most visited parts of the city. But some of the strongest and smartest Africans built Savannah, and they left their marks everywhere. While it may not be easy to find, there's always an elder or two around who knows who left the mark and what it means. So mystical, right? Yet, that's who we are.

We've always been entranced with spirits, magic and mystery. I thought that would be a hindrance to this research, and I couldn't write a book with only questions. I needed answers too. I feared I wouldn't ever find the answers to the questions that I asked. But I was wrong. As the saying goes, when the student is ready, the teacher appears. More than 19 teachers, elders particularly, showed up for me. They trusted me and, more importantly, they wanted to tell the stories. Through those narratives, a new world opened up for me.

That new world shed light on the fact that narrowing black history down to just a few names is an insult. By the time Martin Luther King, Jr. arrived in the city, black Savannah had already made hundreds of miles of progress. Martin was inspired by that progress, by the leaders and the foot soldiers who were already doing the work. Ms. Madie refused to sit down long before she knew about a Rosa Parks. It's important to remember the names, but, more importantly, I think, is to remember the stories. How we fought and how we continue to fight for our voice, our rights, and our freedom, while making it look, sound, and taste so beautiful, is why I wanted to write this book. We have risen, regardless of the people and policies that have tried to keep us down.

Yet, black history ain't just resistance and our fight against that resistance. It's definitely pivotal, but to narrow our history down to our relationship to racism, sexism, and all of its oppressive branches is also offensive. It's deeper than that. As my elders reminisced on W.W. Law, Hosea Williams, and Piccolo, it reminded me not to just see these men as activists but as human beings. Malcolm X wasn't just a freedom fighter. He was a father, husband, son and brother who had hobbies outside of the movement.

That's something that I hope *Krak Teet* accomplished—showing that we fought (and we still fight) hard, but that's not the totality of who we are as a people. Nor is that solely what our people should be celebrated for. When I'm moderating or speaking on a panel, I thoroughly enjoy answering questions. When in attendance, I equally enjoy asking questions. One of my favorite questions to ask is "What did you enjoy doing when you were 8 and when you were 18?" Most recently, I asked Dr. Carla Hayden, the current (and first black and first woman) Librarian of Congress, this question. She loved reading at eight and she didn't even want to share her 18-year-old version of a good time, which made the room cut up laughing. It made her human again. It made her relatable. I saw myself in her.

There's a lot of value in seeing ourselves in one another—in our elders, our ancestors, our peers, and even younger generations. When see yourself in someone, you have more compassion towards them, you respect them, and you're open to listening to them. As we know, when we listen we learn. And the best subject to learn about is yourself as a person and as a people. It's important for the youth, especially, to know that black people in Savannah, in America, and all over the world are innately tenacious and independent. When we needed a school, Susie King Taylor opened her home. When we needed homes, Tin City was built. When we needed our own bank, Wage Earners was built. When we needed our own church, First African Baptist was built. A hospital? McKane hospital turned Charity. A library? Carnegie. Clothing stores and restaurants? Built those too. Our tradition is not waiting on handouts or approval. It's building our own.

Another tradition is togetherness. According to General Cope, an elder I met at St. Matthew's Episcopal Church, we were closer when we had less. If you needed a ride, just ask. Flour, just knock. Your children were mine too, as were your grandparents. We were a village, woven together with respect and understanding. That's not to say that we were perfect and didn't harm one another. I'm not overlooking that, just focusing on the overarching village approach. Got the more we were looking for—more money and options— and we've forgotten how to make time for each other. We're coming back around though. That united part of our history is repeating itself, slowly but surely.

Nelson Mandela said that moving forward as a people requires the wisdom of the elders and the energy of the youth. The youth's energy is on the radio, on the television, in the magazines, up and down the street, and on the news. Elder wisdom, however, is our greatest untapped resource. It's present, but the demand for it is lacking. And we need it now more than ever.

KRAK TEET:

"Where a mentor invites the genius of a youth to come out of its hiding, an elder blesses that genius, thereby allowing it to serve efficiently the greater good." -Malidoma Patrice Some

As much as our elders need us, we need them too! An interdependent, multigenerational complex community enriches our existence. It deepens our sense of identity, our sense of purpose, and our sense of belonging–all of which are necessary ingredients in having pride in who you are and where you're from.

Ms. Madie said, "To tell you the truth, we not completely free yet. When you boil it all down, things are a whole lot better, but we still have a ways to go to be equal." To improve the future, you have to study the past. You have to look at the harm that has been done, how the people responded to that harm, and which of those responses worked in our favor. You have to give the microphone to those who were there, those who remember. It's the responsibility of next generations to carry those memories. Those stories are not just interesting tidbits; they're maps.

Krak Teet also preserves a language and way of life that would otherwise die with its owners. Culture constantly evolves. The Gullah Geechee spoken today is not the same as it was ten, twenty, or fifty years ago. The way it's spoken in Savannah isn't the same as that of Sapelo, Jacksonville, or Charleston. The same can be said for how we treat our injuries and illnesses, how we prepare our meals, and raise our families. It's important to hold onto these traditions. They are our history, our roots, and our inspiration.

On the subject of inspiration, I hope to also inspire locals of Savannah and everywhere else to see history in real-time. Black history ain't just Harriet, Martin, Rosa, and Malcolm. It's your grandma, your daddy, and YOU. It's who you are and who we are. What we struggle with and what we celebrate. It's how we survive. Savannah's landscape is changing fast. The demographics of historically black neighborhoods and districts in Savannah and all over the world are shifting. So take pictures, record the stories, and document your own memories. Write it. Paint it. Film it. Perform it. Krak e teet and tell your story.

REFERENCES

https://georgiahistory.com/marker-monday-the-georgia-infirmary/

Chen, Linda. "Georgia's First Black Police Officer." *GPB*, 3 May 2016, www.gpbnews.org/post/georgias-first-black-police-officer.

Civil Rights Organization. "School Desegregation and Equal Educational Opportunity." 2001. *Civil Rights 101*. 10 May 2017. <http://www.civilrights.org/resources/civilrights101/desegregation.html>.

Coon, Dean. "Time Travel: Why did Sherman spare Savannah?" Savannah Now, 23 May 2014, savannahnow.com/column-accent/2014-05-23/time-travel-why-did-sherman-spare-savannah.

Epstein, Rebecca, et al. *Girlhood Interrupted: The Erasure of Black Girls' Childhood.*

Georgetown Law Center on Poverty and Inequality, 2018.

Few, Jenel. "Savannah Civil Rights Activist 'Piccolo' Pierce Dies." *Savannah Now*, 16 Dec. 2011, www.savannahnow.com/article/20111216/NEWS/312169821.

Georgia Writer's Project. *Drums and Shadows: Survival Studies Among the Georgia Coastal Negroes*. Athens: University of Georgia Press, 1986.

Giesen, James C. *Sharecropping*. 8 August 2016. 12 May 2017. <http://www.georgiaencyclopedia.org/articles/history-archaeology/sharecropping>.

Grant, Donald L. *The Way It Was in the South: The Black Experience in Georgia*. Athens, GA: University of Georgia Press, 2001.

Hale, Grace Elizabeth. "When Jim Crow Drank Coke." *The New York Times,* 29 Jan. 2013, www.nytimes.com/2013/01/29/opinion/when-jim-crow-drank-coke.html.

"History." Imperial Sugar Company. 2019. http://www.imperialsugarcompany.com/history/.

Hoskins, Charles. *W. W. Law and His People*. Savannah: The Gullah Press, 2013.

James, William A. *The Skin Color Syndrome Among African-Americans*. Lincoln: iUniverse, 2003.

Kordas, Ann (2016) "Hex Workers: African American Women, Hoodoo, and Power in the Nineteenth- and Early Twentieth-Century U.S.," *The Journal of Traditions & Beliefs*: Vol. 3, Article 8.
Available at: https://engagedscholarship.csuohio.edu/jtb/vol3/iss1/8

Kramer, Lloyd. "James Baldwin in Paris: Exile, Multiculturalism and the Public Intellectual." Historical

REFERENCES

Reflections / Réflexions Historiques, vol. 27, no. 1, 2001, pp. 27–47. JSTOR, www.jstor.org/stable/41299193.

Monroe, Kristopher. "Work of Savannah's James 'Double Dutch' Kimble Is an Overlooked Treasure." Savannah Now, 3 Sept. 2016, www.savannahnow.com/accent-column/2016 09-03/savartscene-work-savannahs-james-double-dutch-kimble-overlooked-treasure.

Morgan, Philip. *African American Life in the Georgia Lowcountry*. Athens: University of Georgia Press, 2010.

Parker, Kim, et al. "6 facts about the U.S. military and its changing demographics." Pew Research Center, 13 Apr. 2017, www.pewresearch.org/fact-tank/2017/04/13/6-facts-about-the-u-s-military-and-its-changing-demographics/

Perdue, Robert Eugene. *The Negro in Savannah, 1865-1900*. Exposition Press, 1973.

Smitherman, Lynn, et al. "The Use of Folk Remedies Among Children in an Urban Black Community: Remedies for Fever, Colic, and Teething." *American Academy of Pediatrics*, vol. 115, no. 3, Mar. 2005.

Stodghill, Ron. "Savannah, Both Sides." The New York Times, 3 Oct. 2014, www.nytimes.com/2014/10/05/travel/savannah-both-sides.html.

Vogel, Steve. "Black GIs Get Belated Recognition." The Washington Post, 6 Nov. 2000, www.washingtonpost.com/archive/local/2000/11/06/black-gis-get-belated-

recognition/1361da38-4a0c-4ce7-a13b-7490765e6b81/?
utm_term=.63646d769eee.

Ware, Gabrielle. *Savannah Residents Remember Frogtown And Old West Broad Street*. 13
October 2015. <http://www.gpb.org/news/2015/10/13/savannah-residents-remember-frogtown-and-old-west-broad-street>.

Westmacott, Richard Noble. *African-American Gardens and Yards in the Rural South*.
University of Tennessee Press, 1992.

Wilkerson, Isabel. *The Warmth of Other Suns: the Epic Story of Americas Great Migration*.
Vintage Books, 2016.

Made in the USA
Middletown, DE
13 August 2023

36669870R00128